Not Quite American?

In 1975 Dr. E. Bud Edmondson of Longview, Texas, began an endowment fund at Baylor University to honor his father, Mr. Charles S. B. Edmondson. Dr. Edmondson's intent was to have the proceeds from the fund used to bring to the University outstanding historians who could synthesize, interpret, and communicate history in such a way as to make the past relevant to the present generation.

Baylor University and the Waco community are grateful to Dr. Edmondson for his generosity in establishing the CHARLES EDMONDSON HISTORICAL LECTURES.

— — —

This volume is Edmondson lecture twenty-six.

— — —

The views expressed in these lectures are those of the author and do not necessarily reflect the position of Baylor University or Baylor University Press.

Library of Congress Control Number: 2004105427
International Standard Book Number: 1-932792-05-8

Printed in the United States of America on acid-free paper

Not Quite American?

The Shaping of Arab and Muslim Identity in the United States

Yvonne Yazbeck Haddad

B

Baylor University Press
Waco, Texas USA

Not Quite American?

The al-Qaeda attacks of September 11, 2001 on the World Trade Center and the Pentagon are repeatedly depicted as having "changed America forever." Whether or not such hyperbole is completely justified, there can be little doubt of the reverberations of the event in all spheres of American life in general and the lives of Muslims and Arabs living in the United States in particular. The questions that future scholars will have to investigate include such queries as: whether the attacks had a lasting effect on Arabs and Muslims and their integration and assimilation in the United States? What permanent impact, if any, will they have on the unfolding of the articulation of Islam in the American public square? Certainly the United States government is currently attempting to play an important role in such a reformulation of Islam by its high intensity attempts to identify, might one even say create a "moderate Islam," one that is definitively different from that espoused by those who perpetrated the attacks and justified their actions by reference to the religion of Islam.

There are no accurate figures for the number of Muslims in the United States. Neither the census data, nor the records of the Immigration and Naturalization Service, provide any information on religious affiliation of citizens or immigrants. Consequently, there exists a great disparity in the estimates of their number in the United States. The estimates range between two million, as published by the B'nai Brith, and as many as eleven million, as reported by Warith Deen Muhammed, leader of the Muslim

1

American Society (MAS), the largest African-American Muslim organization. The Council on American Islamic Relations (CAIR) reports in all of its communiqués that there are seven million Muslims in the United States. While the numbers are contested, it is generally agreed that they are significant. The larger the community, Muslims believe, the bigger its potential impact in the political arena and influence on policy. The figures appear to be of similar importance to some in the Jewish community who started over a decade ago warning about the "imminent threat" of Muslim presence in America.[1]

An estimated three million Arabic-speaking people (and their descendents, a few of whom are in their sixth generation) now live in the United States, constituting about one percent of the population, the majority having arrived during the last third of the twentieth century. The community is still in the process of being formed and reformed as policies by the American government regulate the flow of immigrants from the Arab world. Legislation limiting immigration, as well as American foreign policy and the prevailing American prejudice against Arabs, Muslims, and Islam, has at times accelerated and at other times impeded the integration and assimilation of the community into American society.

The Arab community in the United States is noted for its diversity, which is evident in its ethnic, racial, linguistic, religious, sectarian, tribal, and national identities. Today Arab-Americans are dispersed throughout the United States; two thirds of them living in ten states, with 33% living in California, New York, and Michigan. They appear to favor urban areas as about half of them (48%) live in twenty large metropolitan areas with the highest concentrations in Los Angeles, Detroit, New York, Chicago, and Washington, D.C. About a quarter of them (23%) are Muslims (Sunni, Shi'ites, and Druze) and constitute a minority within the Arab-American community, the majority of whom are Christian[2]

[1] Daniel Pipes, "The Muslims are Coming! The Muslims are Coming!" *National Review*, November 19, 1990: 28–31; Martin Kramer, "Islam vs. Democracy," *Commentary* 95.1 (1993): 35–42.

[2] The Christian communities are remnants of early Christian churches. Among those who identify their churches as "Orthodox," for example, are of Byzantine, Assyrian, Jacobite, Coptic, and Gregorian rites. Each one of these

with a small Jewish minority.[3] They are also a minority (25%) within the Muslim-American community, which includes an estimated 33% South Asians and 30% African-Americans.[4]

The Arabic-Speaking Immigrants of the United States

A few Muslim males from the Syrian Province of the Ottoman Empire (today's Syria, Lebanon, Jordan Palestine/Israel) began arriving in the United States in the 1870s. They were rural migrant laborers hoping to make money and return to live in their homelands.[5] Their success, the deteriorating economy in the Middle East, and the subsequent famine precipitated by World War I, brought about 4,300 additional Muslims to the United

---

churches has its Catholic Uniate counterpart, those who have established fealty to the Vatican. More recently, Arab countries have seen the establishment of new churches representing Protestant denominations (predominantly Anglican and Presbyterian) with smaller Lutheran, Baptist, Jehovah Witnesses, Pentecostals, and other evangelical and sectarian Christian churches. It is estimated that Catholics (Roman Catholic, Maronite, and Melkite) constitute 42%, Orthodox (Antiochian, Syrian, Greek, and Coptic) 23%, and Protestants (Episcopalians, Baptist and Presbyterian) 12%. *http://www.aaiusa.org/demographics.htm# Religion3.*

[3] See for example: Walter B. Zenner, "The Syrian Jews of Brooklyn," in *A Community of Many Worlds: Arab Americans in New York City*, ed. Kathleen Benson and Philip M. Kayal (Syracuse: Syracuse University Press, 2002) 156–69; Dina Dahbany-Miraglia, "American Yemenite Jewish Interethnic Strategies," in *Persistence and Flexibility: Anthropological Perspectives on the American Jewish Experience*, ed. Walter B. Zenner (Albany: State University of New York Press, 1988) 63–78; Sephardic Archives, *The Spirit of Aleppo Syrian Jewish Immigrant Life in New York, 1890–1939* (Brooklyn, NY, 1986).

[4] It is estimated that 3.4% are from Sub-Saharan Africa, 2.1% European, 1.6% white American converts, 1.3% Southeast Asians, 1.2% Caribbean, 1.1% Turkish, 0.7% Iranian, and 0.6% Hispanic. *http://usinfo.state.gov/products/pub/ muslimlife.*

[5] Alixa Neff, *Becoming American: The Early Arab Immigrant Experience* (Carbondale: Southern Illinois University Press, 1985); E. Hagopian and A. Paden eds., *The Arab-Americans: Studies in Assimilation* (Wilmette, IL: Medina University Press International, 1969); Barbara Aswad, *Arabic-Speaking Communities in American Cities* (New York: Center for Migration Studies, 1984); Eric Hoogland, ed., *Crossing the Waters: Arabic-Speaking Immigrants in the United States before 1940* (Washington, D.C.: Smithsonian Institution Press, 1987).

States between 1899 and 1914.[6] The flow of immigration was interrupted during World War I. Subsequently, it was curtailed by the National Origin Act of 1924 that reduced the quota by restricting the number of immigrants from the Middle East to 100 persons per year.

The early immigrants were classified by the officials of the Immigration and Naturalization Service (INS) as coming from "Turkey in Asia." These immigrants resented the Turkish designation, since many were running away from Ottoman conscription and oppression, as well as the Asia designation since it excluded them from becoming citizens. By1899, the INS began to add the sub-category of "Syrians" to their registration.[7] That became the identity of choice, as argued by Philip Hitti in his *The Syrians in America*,[8] who insisted that Syrians were distinct from the Turks and have made great contributions to human civilization. Among themselves, they talked about being "wlad 'Arab," (children of Arabs), a reference to the language they spoke.

The early Muslim immigrants to the United States from Greater Syria were few in number. They came to the United States when racism and nativism were paramount, when "Anglo conformity" was promoted as the norm for citizenship and the Protestant establishment determined what is American. Like the millions of immigrants who passed through Ellis Island, they followed the patterns of integration and assimilation that refashioned them into American citizens. Their names were anglicized, Muhammad became Mo, Rashid became Dick, Mojahid became Mark, and Ali was recognized as Al. They dug ditches, laid down railroad tracks, peddled, and later opened grocery stores and other businesses that catered to ethnic needs. Their children went to public schools and worked in factories. They enlisted in the

---

[6] Kathleen Moore, *al-Mughtaribun: American Law and the Transformation of Muslim Life in the United States* (Albany: State University of New York Press, 1995); Ian Haney-López, *White by Law: The Legal Construction of Race* (New York: New York University Press, 1996).

[7] Salloum A. Mokarzel, "Can We Retain our Heritage: A Call to Form a Federation of Syrian Societies," *Syrian World*, November 1928: 36–40.

[8] Philip Khuri Hitti, *The Syrians in America* (New York: George H. Doran Co., 1924).

American military during the First and Second World Wars and served with distinction.

The second wave of immigrants came after the end of World War II, when the United States assumed responsibility for the security of the oil fields in the Middle East, and recruited students from the newly independent Arab states to study at American universities with the expectation that once they returned to their home countries they would constitute an important asset to United States interests. They were predominantly of middle and upper class urban backgrounds with the intimate experience of living in pluralistic settings. A large number were graduates of foreign educational institutions run by secular and missionary groups in the Arab world. Their instruction had been primarily in foreign languages and in western curricula: American, British, French, German, and Russian. Two thirds of the students married American wives. A large number of them decided to settle in the United States. By 1961, when Abdo A. Elkholy published his study on Arab-Muslims in Detroit, Michigan and Toledo, Ohio, he estimated that the total number of Muslims of Arab origin in the United States was 78,000, the majority of whom were from Lebanon. The other estimated 30,000 were from Eastern Europe (Albania and Yugoslavia), Pakistan, Turkey, with a few Tatars from the Soviet Union.[9]

The revocation of the Asia Exclusion Act in 1965 dramatically altered the constituency of the Muslim population of the United States. It brought immigrants from all areas of the Arab and Muslim world. The new immigrants were more representative of the ethnic, national, and religious diversity of the Muslim world. They included a large number of highly educated, socially mobile, professional Muslims—part of the Arab and South Asian "brain drain"—and more women. Meanwhile, the opening of the doors of emigration, the changes in immigration laws, and the lottery system that gave visas to winners from all over the world, brought a different "kind" of immigrant. All social and economic classes from villages, towns, and cities stretching from Morocco to

[9] Abdo A. Elkholy, *The Arab Moslems in the United States: Religion and Assimilation* (New Haven: College and University Press, 1966) 24.

Yemen were represented. The majority of new Muslim immigrants came from the subcontinent of Asia: India, Pakistan, and Bangladesh. The latest arrivals included a substantial number of refugees from countries wrenched by civil wars and often suffering the results of western exploitation. Some have called them the "collateral damage" of American foreign policies in such countries as Algeria, Iraq, Lebanon, Somalia, Palestine, and elsewhere. Among them were some of the poorest of the dispossessed, with little or no formal education. They have been more concerned about survival than issues of identity and assimilation. Along with the refugees were those seeking political asylum from Algeria, Libya, Tunisia, and other autocratic regimes.

The "Arab" Muslims of the United States reflect the religious and sectarian divisions of the population of the Arab world. The largest group is Sunni. The percentage of the Shi'ite population in the United States is presumed to be larger than what obtains in the Arab world, due to the fact that their areas of residence were devastated by war (especially Southern Iraq and Lebanon). The Shi'ites include: Ithna 'Asharis (or Ja 'faris) from Iraq, Lebanon, and Syria; Isma'ilis from Syria; Zaidis from Yemen; 'Alawis from Lebanon and Syria; and Druze from Israel, Lebanon, Palestine, and Syria. All of these groups have established their distinctive community organizations in the United States. They generally affirm that there are no differences between Shi'ites and Sunnis. But while they may worship in the same mosque, there have been incidents of tension over whether members of the two communities can intermarry, or whether one group can perform the burial prayer over a deceased person from the other.

Immigrants from the Arab world reflect also the variety of minority and ethnic communities that constitute the populations of these nations including Armenians, Assyrians, Chechens, Circassians, Kurds, and Turcomans, who have been subjected to the Arabization programs of Arab governments since their independence. Many in these groups tend to dissociate themselves from Arab identity once they emigrate. Some do identify as Arabs or as Arab-Americans, others have set up lobbies in Washington, collaborating with pro-Israeli groups, and are engaged in defaming Arab nations. The Arabic language may seem to be the strongest common bond among Arabs and an initial indicator of ethnic identity. However, the variety of dialects makes it difficult, for example, for Maghrebis (North Africans) and Mashreqis (from the Levant and the Arabian Peninsula) to communicate. For most the common language is English.

Those who emigrated in the second half of the twentieth century brought with them diverse national identities, developed by the nation state to inspire their loyal citizens so they would defend national security against outside enemies. For immigrants, their attachments to these national identities are continually tested by events in their home countries and by American foreign policy towards their countries. Such home ties became strained during the Gulf War in 1990–91 when Gulf Arabs questioned the authenticity of the "Arabness" among citizens of the northern states (Egypt, Jordan, Morocco, Palestine, Syria, and Tunisia) who opposed Saudi Arabian and American retribution against Saddam Hussein, and dismissed them as "Arabized" peoples who did not understand the threat that Saddam's military posed to the Gulf states. At the same time, some Arabs of the northern tier criticized Gulf Arabs as greedy and gullible, and accused them of contributing to the disempowerment of the Arab people in their willingness to spend tens of billions of dollars to support American destruction of Iraq and to empower Israel in the process.

Not all Arabs living in the United States are immigrants. Temporary residents appear to have some influence on immigrants as they interact with them in cultural, social, religious, and political affairs. They include migrant laborers who come from different countries, with the largest number from Yemen.[10] Émigrés, as well as political and religious refugees, have some impact on the assimilation of the Arab immigrants as they focus on events overseas. They live in limbo awaiting a change in the political circumstances in their home countries. A third group are the

---

[10] Nabeel Abraham, "Detroit's Yemeni Workers," *MERIP Reports* 53 (1977): 3–9; Nabeel Abraham, "National and Local Politics: A Study of Political Conflict in the Yemeni Immigrant Community of Detroit, Michigan," diss., University of Michigan, 1978.

thousands of students attending various colleges and universities throughout the United States. Other temporary residents include tourists, business people, and relatives. They also include a large contingent of diplomats to the United States and the United Nations from fifty-six Islamic nations who continue to be active in Arab and Islamic affairs.

Two international Islamic organizations, the Muslim World League (MWL) and the Organization of Islamic Conference (OIC), are recognized by the United Nations as non-governmental organizations and have diplomats in New York City. The Muslim World League had extensive involvement with Muslim organizations in the United States in the 1980s. It organized the Council of Masajid [places of worship] in North America, provided imams from overseas for the leadership of twenty-six mosques, and funded Islamic activity in the United States. Several other Arab nations including Egypt, Iraq, Libya, Kuwait, Qatar, and the United Arab Emirates have funded publications and mosque constructions, among other projects.

Becoming American

There are very few studies that document the Americanization of Arab-Muslims in the United States. In the late 1950s, Abdo Elkholy attempted to assess the acculturation and assimilation of two Muslim communities after the incubation period of at least a quarter century when immigrants from the Middle East lived in isolation. The immigration quota sysem of the 1920s, the depression of the 1930s, and World War II limited communications and further immigration from the region. Elkholy focused his investigation on whether "adherence to the old religion which differs from the religion prevailing in the adopted culture," and particularly Islam, are an impediment to the assimilation of immigrants of Arab ancestry into the United States. His research demonstrated the invalidity of the theory that religion delays the assimilation of immigrant groups into the new culture. Focusing on the two Arab-American Muslim communities (some of whom were fourth generation) living in Toledo, Ohio and Detroit, Michigan, he concluded that, although the two communities were formed by immigrants arriving at the same time from the same area in Lebanon and were identical ethnically and religiously, the Toledo community was more assimilated and religious.[11]

Elkholy determined that the factor appearing to have the most impact on Arab-Muslims' assimilation was their occupation. The Detroit community was predominantly working class, lived in a ghetto-like environment, maintained traditional perceptions of the family, perpetuated sectarian conflicts, and had virtually no interaction with non-Muslims.[12] In contrast, Elkholy described the Toledo Muslims as liberal, "Americanized by liquor." The members of the Toledo community had higher incomes, largely a result of their engagement in the liquor industry and ownership of 30% of the city's bars.[13] Aware that Islam forbids alcohol, they did not consume alcohol themselves, but rationalized selling it.[14] Although they had lived in disparate areas of the United States before settling in Toledo, they were generally related to one another, displayed a greater harmony between the generations, and appeared to share a common goal of preserving their middle-class social status. Although they attended mosque services, they appeared ignorant of important Islamic prescriptions. For example, they prayed on Sunday in the mosques without performing the required ablutions. They also maintained social relations with Christians, attended social events in churches, and displayed an American flag in the mosque.[15]

Generally ignorant of Islamic prescriptions and ritual, the young members of the Toledo mosque used the building primarily as a social center. "The mosque had thus become not only the place for worship and religious instruction but also the popular place for the youth where American social activities range from dating to mixed dancing." (Of the young people in the survey, 82% did not know that ablutions were prescribed after sex.)[16]

11 Elkholy, *Arab Moslems*, 15–16.
12 Ibid., 18.
13 Ibid., 18.
14 Ibid., 58.
15 Ibid., 34, 37.
16 Ibid., 92.

Elkholy also noted that: "The same loudspeaker which broadcasts the recorded Qur'anic verses before Friday prayer now broadcasts the rock and roll music of the third generation and waltzes for the second."[17]

In Detroit, young Muslims were living through an economic recession. Elkholy disapproved of their leisure activities—their preferred music for dancing was the Lebanese dabkeh[18]—and described them as "scores of idle, jobless young men" who spent their time gambling and fighting between cliques. They were, he went on, engaged in "night life activities to the Moslem 'beat' generation" and were "religiously weak." He attributed their behaviors to authoritarian parents and he saw the mosque as a place for "men" who were "aged and backward.[19]

Elkholy also noted that factors leading other immigrants to assimilate in the United States, such as language acquisition and preference for middle-class areas of residence, were also melding Arab-Muslims into American citizens. He argued that Islam was functioning as an assimilating religion by bringing the communities together as they began to shed their ethnic identities. In fact, he observed that the third generation in Toledo was more religious, while that of Detroit was more nationalistic, and that strong religious affiliation in the Toledo community accelerated, rather than hindered, its assimilation.[20]

A quarter century after Elkholy's study, another study of five Muslim communities, published in 1985, found that acculturation and assimilation were progressing among Muslims despite the influx of a large number of new immigrants from different areas with distinctive identities.[21] The study focused on five groups of Muslim settlers in the United States, four of which had established mosques by the 1930s (Dearborn, Michigan; Toledo, Ohio;

---

[17] Ibid., 33, 37.
[18] Ibid., 33.
[19] Ibid., 90.
[20] Ibid., 69, 95, 98.
[21] Yvonne Yazbeck Haddad and Adair T. Lummis, *Islamic Values in the United States: A Comparative Study* (New York: Oxford University Press, 1987).

Cedar Rapids, Iowa; and Quincy, Massachusetts) and another, comprised primarily by Pakistani immigrants, that had established a new mosque in Rochester, New York. The 1985 survey noted the traditional role of the imam had been transformed even though a few of the imams, who were supported by the Muslim World League, had attempted to replicate the tradition of authority that obtained overseas. In several instances, the imams were overruled by their congregations who had invested the decision-making role in the mosques' elected executive committees. From being a leader of prayer, the imam in the United States had taken on the role of a pastor, providing counseling and instruction in the faith, representing the community to the general public, participating in interfaith activities, and defending the faith.

The 1985 survey found that over two thirds of the Muslims sampled had a graduate degree, making this the best educated Muslim population in the world. Their educational achievement was also well above the national average of the United States. While it is possible that only the highly educated chose to participate in the study, further research revealed that these immigrants placed a great stress on college education as a means of social and economic mobility. One Arab-American in her 60s who grew up in Ohio, reported proudly, "My parents came to this country as illegal immigrants. They were both illiterate, but they worked hard and put all eight children through college."

The immigrant cohort of the fifties came to the United States for higher education, and, as American higher education expanded in the 1960s, a great number became professors at universities. While a significant number of this group became professionals and business people in the United States, it was mostly the immigrants who were admitted on preference visas after 1965 who became doctors and engineers. They brought with them a special enthusiasm for these two professions as they are highly prized in the Arab world as a means to social and economic mobility. Many parents pressured their sons to follow their footsteps. In the middle of the 1990s, the children of this group began to specialize in law, journalism, and the social sciences.

Further trends in Americanization, as noted by Elkholy, included the adoption of values that are contrary to Arab customs, particularly in choosing a marriage partner. Whereas arranged marriages are still in effect in large parts of the Arab world, the Arab-Muslim communities of Detroit and Toledo considered marriage to be a matter of personal choice with courtship emulating American patterns. But, the majority (71%) had married Muslims. Although about half the communities (45% in Toledo, 45% in Detroit) opposed the marriage of females to non-Muslims, Elkholy also found that two thirds of the people interviewed would not oppose interfaith marriages, if the spouses were allowed to practice their faiths.[22] More recently, while arranged marriages have continued to be the norm among the majority of the children of recently arrived immigrants, especially those from small towns and rural areas, new means of matchmaking have been devised, including advertising in ethnic and religious magazines, and through an internet service. On college campuses, many young Arab-Americans have become indistinguishable from their colleagues in that they go to bars, date, drink, and smoke pot.

Elkholy concluded that Muslim women increased their participation in public life as part of their Americanization. He reported that, "The family pattern of these two communities is approximately American. The wife is not merely the equal of her husband; she also dominates the family." Although he noted that wives help their husband in their business ventures, he failed to realize that, in the rural areas of Lebanon, from which these immigrants had come, women had previously played an important part in economic and public life.

The later research survey uncovered an important fact in Dearborn: that women were the primary instigators in establishing the mosque. They not only took the initiative in securing a place for the religious and social activities of the community, but they also raised the funds necessary, through bake sales and door-to-door soliciting. They managed the activities in the mosque

---

[22] Elkholy *Arab Moslems*, 31–32, 70.

facilities, arranging for weddings, receptions, and *haflehs* that included dancing. The influx of new immigrants into Dearborn, primarily Yemeni male migrant laborers, with a different cultural understanding of the role of women in society created a crisis in the community. The Yemenis, who wrested control of the mosque through the courts by arguing that its extra-religious activities were un-Islamic, dispatched the women to the basement, and restricted their access to the mosque through a separate door. Thus the new immigrants attempted to recreate their notion of Muslim society in the American context. Other actors, primarily the recently imported foreign imams, who were hired to run the mosques, attempted to enforce gender segregation. Scandalized by the dancing and social events taking place in the mosque, they insisted the mosque be used exclusively for prayer and religious instruction.

The majority of the Muslim women in the United States during the 1960s did not veil. Veiling was generally perceived as part of the maintenance of old customs, which were already dying out in Middle Eastern urban areas.[23] The 1985 study corroborated Elkholy's findings of Americanization.[24] It found that the degree of strictness in adhering to "Islamic dress" varied from one mosque to another. Some mosques permitted women to attend prayer in knee length skirts and no head coverings, whereas others insisted that women cover all their bodies and in some cases provided them with wraps.[25] The more recent arrival of new immigrants who believed that the covering of the woman's hair is a divine commandment has led to an increase in the number of women voluntarily donning the *hijab*, even though, in many cases, their mothers had never worn one and their grandmothers had cast it away in the 1920s and 1930s. Also recently affecting the role of women is the immigration of Muslims from South Asia who advocate more traditional customs, including even the banning of handshaking between the sexes.[26]

23 Ibid., 70.
24 Haddad and Lummis, *Islamic Values*, 126–27.
25 Ibid., 132.
26 Ibid., 134–36.

Islamic knowledge continued to be restricted to male exper-
tise. Women's religious activity was mostly restricted to "sisters"
groups. Although women did lead study circles that focused on
Islamic knowledge and the teachings of the Qur'an, these were
generally conducted in private homes. By the 1990s, some
Muslim women had begun to make their contributions to public
life as academics, teachers, and researchers. Some were working
through the Islamic historical and juridical sciences to reinterpret
and provide new insights into Islamic knowledge and had published many studies on the role and status of women in Islam. In
an effort to influence the cultural and social restrictions on
women, some have offered new progressive insights and interpretations grounded in the text of the Qur'an and the example of the
Prophet Muhammad.

Unlike Muslim countries, in the United States mosque attendance is a family affair rather than a strictly male activity. Muslim
women do attend *jum'a* (Friday communal prayers), albeit in
smaller numbers than the Sunday family prayers. In some
mosques, women's allotted space for prayer is located at the back
of the prayer hall behind the men. At other mosques, women are
at the side, often separated by a barrier or a curtain. Occasionally,
women pray in a separate space, such as a basement, a loft, or an
auxiliary room where they can watch the service on closed circuit
television. Most women interviewed found the separation helped
them to concentrate on prayer rather than on members of the
opposite sex.

The "Arab" Experience of America

Who is an Arab? What is an Arab? How does one become an
Arab? These are questions that were hotly debated in the forma-
tive period of the modern Arab nation states during the first half
of the twentieth century and continue to generate a great deal of
discussion. An Arab nationalist identity was proposed as the foundation for a modern state that would consider as Arab all who
speak the Arabic language and identify with Arab history and culture, regardless of whether they are Muslims, Christians, or Jews.

This multi-religious view was promoted primarily by Jews and Christians in an effort to carve out a national identity where religious minorities would be recognized as full citizens. This view was also propagated by some Arabic-speaking Muslims opposing the Young Turks who were seeking to "Turkify" all ethnic and tribal groups resident in the Ottoman Empire. Today, several other meanings may be given to the word "Arab." One, for example, restricts the term to those who are native to the Arabian Peninsula as opposed to those who live in the "Arabized" northern tier (Iraq, Lebanon, Syria, Jordan, Palestine, Egypt, and North Africa). Another much broader definition is based on citizenship in any of the twenty-two Arab states that are members of the Arab League.

Immigrants from the Arab world are, in a manner of speaking, veterans of the struggle to modernize and westernize in the context of the colonial and post-colonial era. In the United States, they perceive a nation that has some very strong institutions, that sees itself as a model democracy, and that welcomes all who choose to share in the American dream. It seems to be a nation that advocates openness and pluralism as foundational principles of its polity. But somewhere behind these principles lurks the possibility of an anti-Saracen heritage that is as anti-Arab and anti-Muslim as it is anti-Semitic, if not more so.[27] Indeed, surveys of the media have documented the demonization of Arabs, Islam, and Muslims as the monolithic "outsiders," the essential "other," whose beliefs and customs are characterized as inferior, barbaric, sexist, and irrational—values worthy of repeated condemnation and eradication.[28]

[27] John V. Tolan, *Saracens: Islam in the Medieval European Imagination* (New York: Columbia University Press, 2002); Norman Daniel, *Islam and the West: The Making of an Image* (Oxford: One World, 1993); V. G. Kiernan, *The Lords of Human Kind: European Attitudes to the Outside World in the Imperial Age* (London: Pelican, 1972); Robert Young, *White Mythologies: Writing History and the West* (London: Routledge, 1990).

[28] Karim H. Karim, *Islamic Peril: Media and Global Violence* (Montreal: Black Rose Books, 2000); Edward Said, *Covering Islam: How the Media and the Experts Determine How We See the Rest of the World* (New York: Vantage Books, 1997); Abbas Malek, *Newsmedia and Foreign Relations: A Multi-faceted Perspective* (Norwood, NJ: Ablex Publishing 1996); William J. Griswald, *The Image of the*

Arab-American identity has been honed and reshaped by the immigrants themselves in response to American attitudes and policies towards them as well as their original homeland. This identity is also fashioned by the immigrants' local American experiences, the place in which they settle, their relations with older generations of immigrants, the reception and treatment they endure in their new environment, the diversity of the community with which they associate, their involvement in organized religion, and attendance at ethnic or integrated mosques. Increasingly, it has also been profoundly influenced by American prejudice and hostility towards Arabs and Muslims, both real and perceived.

Arab-Americans have attempted to synthesize their experiences of America with the Arab and Muslim experience of a dominant "West" during the history of European colonial expansion and subjugation of the Muslim world beginning in the sixteenth century and lasting through the first half of the twentieth century. Western domination of Arab nations has been perceived as continuing through American hegemony and intervention in the area since the 1950s, and as manifest today in what Arabs see as the American support of Israeli colonial and expansionist policies in Palestine and the surrounding Arab states. American support for autocratic regimes that appear to be clients of American interests, and the recent American declared war on terrorism, implemented through regime change in Afghanistan and Iraq and widely perceived by the Arab and Muslim world as a war on Islam, appear to fit the same pattern.

Middle East in Secondary School Textbooks (New York: Middle East Studies Association of North America, 1975); Samir Ahmad Jarrar, "Images of the Arabs in United States Secondary School Textbooks," diss., Florida State University, 1976; Ayad al-Qazzaz, "Images of the Arabs in American Social Science Textbooks," in *Arabs in America: Myths and Realities*, ed. Baha Abu Laban and Faith T. Ziadeh (Willmette, IL: Medina University Press International, 1975); Glenn Perry, "Treatment of the Middle East in American High School Textbooks," *Journal of Palestine Studies* 4.3 (1975): 46–58.

The Encounter with Zionism

The early immigrants from the Middle East were concerned about the fate of their relatives back home in the aftermath of World War I. A few lobbied the American government to help create the Arab state promised in the Faisal-McMahon Correspondence, and some Maronites worked for the creation of Greater Lebanon. However, the majority of immigrants did not appear to be interested in political activity. Rather, most of their early organizations were social, ethnic, or religious in nature.

The Syrian and Lebanese American Federation of the Eastern States was formed in Boston. Its membership included a variety of organizations that were social clubs, cultural groups, and charitable organizations. In 1932, the National Association of Syrian and Lebanese-American Organizations was formed and later the National Association of Federations. In the early 1950s, the Federation sponsored a convention in Lebanon to foster goodwill among the United States, Syria, and Lebanon. "During the life of the federation movement up until the 1960s, there was little real interest in the Middle East question by the majority of the member groups, although convention resolutions did often express feelings by the leadership that Zionism was a threat to Arab and American relations and was not in the best interest of the United States." There is little evidence that the majority of the membership, a substantial number of whom were second and third generations, had any awareness of events overseas or the geography of the Middle East. Some of them had even contributed to the United Jewish Appeal.[29] The National Association of Federations ceased to exist in the late 1950s and early 1960s.

By the 1940s, the Arabic-speaking immigrants in the United States began to feel uncomfortable as the Zionist campaign for the recognition and support for the State of Israel became intense. Among the slogans adopted by the Zionists were: "A land without

---

[29] Elaine Hagopian, "Minority Rights in a Nation State: The Nixon Administration's Campaign against Arab-Americans," *Journal of Palestine Studies* 5:1/2 (1975–76): 97–114.

a people for a people without a land."[30] The immigrants knew
better. Not only was Palestine populated with Palestinians, both
Christian and Muslim, but some of the immigrants still had relatives and friends in Haifa, Jaffa, Ramallah, Beit Jala, Jerusalem,
the Galilee, and elsewhere. The most galling Zionist slogan that
had a far-reaching influence on Arabs openly solicited funds for
the eradication of Arabs: "Pay a dollar, kill an Arab." It had a great
impact on Sayyid Qutb, an Egyptian author on a scholarship in
the United States between 1949 and 1951. An agnostic, he
returned home totally disillusioned with the United States, which
he characterized as racist anti-Arab, anti-Muslim. Back in Egypt,
he became active in the Muslim Brotherhood movement and
became the greatest advocate of Islamism as an alternative to capitalism and communism, as a system that guaranteed justice and
equality, where there is no distinction based on color or national
identity.

By the 1950s, the impact of the conflict in the Middle East on
the Muslim community in Detroit was palpable. Elkholy noted
that they emphasized that they were Arab, regardless of whether
they emigrated from Lebanon, Iraq, Syria, or Yemen.[31] One inter-
viewee told Elkholy that: "Wherever a party is opened in the
name of the Prophet, no one is particularly moved. If it is opened
in the name of God, no one cares either. But the name of Gamal
Abdel-Nasser electrifies the hall."[32] He attributed the phe-
nomenon to the "continuing threat posed by the existence of
Israel and Nasser's resistance to Israel and the Western political
pressure."[33]

A substantial number of the new Muslim immigrants brought
a different identity, one fashioned by the devastating experience of
the Israeli attack of 1967 and the catastrophic Arab defeat (*al-
Nakba*), the failed Arab counterattack in 1973, the Israeli invasion
of Lebanon in 1982, and the massacres of Sabra and Shatila in

[30] Michael Palumbo, "Land Without a People," *http://www.geocities.com/
CapitolHill/Senate/7891Palumbo_chtr1.html, 4.*
[31] Elkholy, *Arab Moslems*, 18.
[32] Ibid., 48.
[33] Ibid., 48–49.

1983. The Lebanese civil war, in which the Maronite Christians colluded with Israel against the Palestinians, led to Muslim distrust of Arab Christians. The new immigrants represented a generation that had wearied of Arab nationalism perceived to have failed to deliver on the hopes of Arab people for justice for the Palestinian people, for parity with the west, and for input into the world order. Their identity was shaped by the ideology that was beginning to sweep across the Arab world, one that affirmed religious identity as a means of resistance to fundamentalist secularism, promoted by a variety of regimes in the Middle East, as well as hegemonic "Judeo-Christianity," experienced as the "dominance of expansionist Israel as supported and empowered by Western nations." They had come to subscribe to some form of Islamic identity, and included a small minority who favored "Islamism" as the only way to foster unity and strength to combat what is perceived as incessant efforts to undermine Islam and Muslims.

Those who came in the 1980s had witnessed the Iranian revolution of 1979 that demonstrated the power of Islamic identity in mobilizing the population to dethrone the shah, "the mightiest of tyrants," who was considered a lackey of the United States and Israel. These experiences generated a growing consensus that Arab nationalist identity was a colonial construct devised to divide the Muslims and separate them into ethnic, racial, and language groups in order to dominate them. The new understanding was that only an Islamic identity, creating solidarity with other Muslim nations, can provide the necessary resources to fight for Muslim causes. The Arab states, went this line of thinking, would be empowered by the larger Muslim support from Indonesia, Pakistan, and elsewhere.

The prevailing American hostility towards Arabs during the 1967 Israeli pre-emptive strike against Egypt, Syria, and Jordan, and the immigrants' awareness of the ignorance of the American public about the facts of the conflict in the Middle East, led to the formation of the first organization to assume a hyphenated identity and coin the term "Arab-American." The Association of Arab-American University Graduates, (AAUG) was formed in

1967 by graduate students, professionals, university professors, lawyers, doctors, and veterans of the Organization of Arab Students (OAS). It reflected an Arab nationalist ideology and made no distinction among members based on religious affiliation or national origin. It placed special emphasis on production of knowledge and the education of both its membership, as well as the American public about the Arab world.

They immediately became the target of the Zionist lobby, which began to portray Arab activists as spies and propagandists for foreign interests.[34] The *Near East Report* devoted several issues in 1969 to the "alleged threat" of the presence of Arabs in the United States. The expressed concern was over Arab "propaganda" on American campuses. To its editors, "the Arab viewpoint reaching American ears was of equal concern as alleged security threats."[35] It warned Americans that Arab students may harbor *fedayeen* among them and that Arabs were trying to infiltrate leftist organizations. Other lobby groups became active in silencing professors of Middle Eastern Studies on American campuses, asking for the elimination of funding for centers supported by Title VI to provide experts in area studies for government services. The lobby also targeted politicians who questioned American support of Israel, including Senator Percy of Illinois and Senator Fulbright of Arkansas, both of whom were perceived to have lost their elections because of the funding of their opponents from the Israeli lobby.[36]

Other Arab-American organizations were established by the second and third generations, veterans of the earlier federations. They were formed to defend the civil and political rights of the

[34] Helen Hatab Samhan, "Politics and Exclusion: The Arab American Experience," *Journal of Palestine Studies* 16.2 (1987): 16; Hatem I. Hussaini, "The Impact of the Arab-Israeli Conflict on Arab Communities in the United States," in *Settler Regimes in Africa and the Arab World: The Illusion of Endurance*, ed. Ibrahim Abu-Lughod and Baha Abu-Laban (Wilmette, IL: The Medina University Press International, 1974); *Near East Report*, May 14, 1969 and October 29, 1969. Hagopian, "Minority Rights," 101.

[35] Michael R. Fischbach, "Government Pressure Against Arabs in the United States," *Journal of Palestine Studies* 14.3 (1985): 89.

[36] For additional details, see Paul Findley, *They Dare Speak Out: People and Institutions Confront Israel's Lobby* (Chicago: Lawrence Hill Books, 1989).

community and in response to American government policies that targeted Arab-Americans. Operation Boulder was launched in 1972 by the Nixon administration after the massacre of Israeli athletes at Munich. The United States government sought the help of the Israeli government and pro-Israeli organizations in the United States to spy on the community.[37] It shared intelligence with the Israeli government and appropriated the Israeli designation of "Arabs as terrorists."[38] The FBI began to compile dossiers on organizations and on members of the community, by tapping their telephones and gathering information about their political ideas, the journals to which they subscribed and their circle of friends.[39] Operation Boulder featured intimidation by FBI agents, the restriction of movement by Arabs in the United States, and the deportation of hundreds on technical irregularities. Immigration from the Arab world was restricted. Although Operation Boulder officially came to an end in 1975, harassment of politically active Arab-Americans continued, with the apparent purpose of intimidating the community and discouraging Arab political activity. This massive scrutiny did not result in identifying any anti-American activities.[40]

Other government actions and policies increased the marginalization of Arab-Americans and heightened their anxiety. Utilizing the Freedom of Information Act, the Arab community learned that in 1986 the American administration was considering the use of two military compounds in the South for the possible internment of Arabs and Iranians, as had been done to the Japanese during World War II. They were shocked by the way that anti-Arab perceptions were encouraged by the ABSCAM[41]

[37] *The New York Times*, May 24, 1973; *Washington Post*, October 15, 1972.

[38] Fischbach, "Government Pressure," 87–100.

[39] M. C. Bassiouni, ed., "The Civil Rights of Arab-Americans: 'The Special Measures'," Information paper #10 (Belmont, MA: Association of Arab-American University Graduates, 1974); Hagopian, "Minority Rights," 102.

[40] Abdeen Jabara, "The FBI and the Civil Rights of Arab-Americans," *ADC Issues* no. 5 (n.d.): 1.

[41] Jack Shaheen, *Abscam: Arabophobia in America* (Washington, D.C.: American-Arab Anti-Discrimination Committee, [1980?]); Jerry J. Berman, "A Public Policy Report," *ACLU Washington Office*, October 10, 1982.

investigation, when FBI agents masqueraded as Arabs in order to bribe members of Congress.

Such events, perceived as a vicious and racially discriminatory campaign against persons of Arab origin, offended the dignity of many Arab-Americans, particularly the American-born of Syrian and Lebanese origin who viewed themselves as loyal and law-abiding Americans[42] and who had fought to defend the United States and its interests and values in World War I and World War II. Second- and third-generation Lebanese-Americans organized the National Association of Arab Americans (NAAA) in 1972. Modeled after the pro-Israel lobby, the American Israel Public Affairs Committee,[43] its leadership, sought to educate Arab-Americans about the political process as well as arrange for them to meet with members of Congress to discuss issues of great concern to the community. In addition, the American-Arab Anti-Discrimination Committee (ADC) was founded by former American-born Senator James Aburezk and James Zoghby, both of Christian Lebanese origin.[44] It was modeled after the ADL (Anti Defamation League) to fight racism, prejudice, and discrimination against Arabs. It is currently the largest grassroots Arab organization, with chapters throughout the United States.

The Arab American Institute (AAI) was established in 1984 when James Zoghby split from the ADC. It encourages Arab-Americans to participate in the American political system, working to get Arab-Americans to vote and to run for office. It has sought to establish Democratic and Republican clubs, such as those active in the presidential campaigns of Jesse Jackson (1988), Gore-Lieberman (2000), and Bush-Cheney (2000). Arab immigrants generally lack experience in political participation, fear the

[42] Ayad al-Qazzaz, "The Arab Lobby: Toward an Arab-American Political Identity," *al-Jadid* 3 (1997): 10.

[43] Jerome Bakst, "Arabvertising: The New Brand of Arab Propaganda," *Times of Israel*, April 1975: 15–23; as referenced in Hagopian, "Minority Rights," 111.

[44] Gregory Orfalea, "Sifting the Ashes: Arab-American Activism During the 1982 Invasion of Lebanon," *Arab Studies Quarterly* 11.2&3 (1989): 207–26.

consequences of political involvement, and have no experience in coalition building. Major political candidates, including George McGovern, Walter Mondale, Joseph Kennedy, and Mayor Goode of Philadelphia, have shunned them and returned their financial contribution because they are perceived as a liability, often out of fear of antagonizing the pro-Israel lobby. Recently, in the 2000 New York senatorial contest, Republican candidate Rick Lazio depicted Arab and Muslim contributions to Hillary Clinton's campaign as "blood-money," which led to her returning the donations. Many in the community feel disenfranchised, given the importance of donations in providing access to elected officials and determining American policies.

All Arab-American organizations were formed by a coalition of Christians and Muslims from the Arab states. What held them together was the shared vision of American stereotyping of Arabs and Muslims and their shared experience and interpretations of events in the Middle East. The organizations were cemented by a perception of Zionist stalking of their activities and intimidation of their speakers, and by a deep commitment to the American democratic process. They expected America to live up to its proclaimed values and placed their trust in the American judicial system and the guarantees of the Constitution and Bill of Rights.

The Muslim Experience of America

Once the pioneer Muslim migrants from the Arab world decided to settle in the United States, they were eager to belong, and in the process they tried to interpret American culture as compatible with Arab concepts of virtue and honor. They emphasized the similarities between Islam and Christianity, for example, the respect Islam has for Jesus and his mother Mary. Early records show that they were dispersed throughout the United States, and initially tended to socialize with Christian and Jewish immigrants from the Arab world. They sent their children to Christian parochial schools in order to imbue their education with ethical values. It was not until the 1930s that they began to have structures dedicated for Islamic services. In communicating with the American public, they tended to talk about the Qur'an as "our bible," the mosque as "our church," the imam as "our minister." Their great-grandchildren are now indistinguishable from other Americans. Their dispersion and isolation, as well as the hardship they went through, led to little organized activity. Some belonged to the Syrian and Lebanese Federations.

Abdullah Igram of Cedar Rapids, Iowa, a veteran of World War II having experienced marginalization in the American military, worked to bring Islam and its adherents into the mainstream by seeking recognition from President Eisenhower. He requested that the religious affiliation of Muslims be recognized by the United States military, which previously left it blank on their "dog tags." In 1953, he called for a general meeting of Muslims, and members from twenty-two different mosques and centers in the United States and Canada participated. The next year they formed the Federation of Islamic Associations in the United States and Canada (FIA). It eventually had a membership of fifty-four mosques and Islamic centers. Reflecting the constituency of the Muslim population in the United States in the 1950s, the majority of the congregations of these mosques were Lebanese.

The immigrants of the 1970s often found the accommodation of the earlier immigrants to American culture too high a price to pay, especially since America began to define itself as Protestant, Catholic, and Jewish. They found the social and spiritual problems of America repugnant, even as they enjoyed America's economic opportunities and freedom of religion, association, and speech. They accused the earlier immigrants of diluting the importance of Islamic traditions, rituals, and distinguishing characteristics. They believed that difference and distinctiveness were a necessary means of affirming a place for Islam. Their conscious religious observances and their publications emphasized the great importance of the manner of prayer, and how women were to dress, walk and talk. Rather than stressing commonalities with American culture and religion they put the emphasis on the differences. They were confident that Islam is the perfect way, and the cure for all that ails America.

Other factors contributed to the development of Islamic institutions in the United States in the 1990s. For one thing, there was a dramatic growth in the number of Muslim immigrants to the United States between 1970 and 1990 creating a larger cohort group of practicing Muslims. Many came from middle and lower middle classes in rural areas and elected to maintain their traditional dress, while finding in mosque institutions a support system that helped them establish networks, find jobs, and companionship.

The Salman Rushdie affair affirmed for Muslim observers the lack of Western sympathy for Islamic sensitivities. They noted that the media emphasized the condemnation of the *Satanic Verses* as a negation of freedom of speech in a country that believes that books should not be censored. However, they also could not help but see that the speech codes of the United States and political correctness have generally frowned on works of fiction that offend Jewish and African-American sensitivities such as *The Protocols of the Elders of Zion* and *Little Black Sambo*. That the American establishment refused to condemn the *Satanic Verses* was seen as yet another example of demonizing Islam and Muslims. For many, it was a signal that they had not arrived as yet.

The last decade of the twentieth century ushered in a new phase in Muslim integration and assimilation into the United States. Several factors coalesced to bring about a major transformation in the Muslim community. The Gulf War of 1990 marked the end of financial support from Saudi Arabia and other Gulf nations. Initially, the withdrawal of support had a devastating effect on Islamic projects in the United States. Both ISNA and FIA shut down for lack of funds to pay their staff. But communal paralysis did not set in. Several of the alumni of the Muslim Student Association welcomed the freedom from dependency and began to work to establish permanent Islamic institutions. In the process, the power shifted from umbrella organizations to decentralized leadership, the independent mosque executive committees. While ISNA reopened with a skeleton staff, its ability to control and guide the progress of Islam nationwide had been greatly diminished. Its journal, *Islamic Horizon*, continues to be distributed nationally, and its annual conventions draw about 30,000 Muslims. It has recently started hosting annual academic conferences on "Islam in America," "Islam in Prisons," and "Islam among Latinos," which provide important insights on the daily life of Muslims in North America.

While the 1980s saw the development of Arab-American organizations interested in public policy, the 1990s brought about several Islamic organizations. The American Muslim Alliance (AMA) was formed in California in 1989 by Agha Saeed. The goal was to empower Muslims to participate in the political process by voting and running for office. Others include: the American Muslim Council (AMC, founded in 1990), the Council on American Islamic Relations (CAIR, 1994), and the Muslim Public Affairs Council (MPAC). Their goals generally paralleled those of the Arab organizations that came into existence in the 1980s since several of the leaders were those organizations' alumni, who saw a growing need to create Islamic institutions to engage the non-Arab Muslims in supporting a variety of political and civil rights issues relevant to the growing Muslim community.

With the election of William Clinton as President of the United States, Muslims perceived a major transformation occur in the political allegiances of government policymakers. Clinton was beholden to the Jewish community because of its extensive support during his campaign. At the urging of Senator Joseph Lieberman, Democrat of Connecticut, the new administration brought twenty-seven activists from the pro-Israeli lobby into the government and placed them in charge of Middle East policy. During his two terms in office, they were able to weave the American-Israel relationship into a seamless entity. It appeared to Muslims and Arabs that American interests in the Middle East were being subsumed under the primary interests of Israel.

At the same time that the foreign policy initiatives of the government were deemed anti-Palestinian and anti-Muslim, the Clinton administration initiated a policy of symbolic inclusion of

American Muslims. Periodically, leaders of the various Muslim organizations were invited to public events and occasionally had an audience with policymakers and talked about their issues. Mrs. Clinton hosted the first *iftar* dinner (the break of the fast of Ramadan) at the Department of State. Although some in the Muslim leadership were enamored by what they perceived as elevation of their status, they were fully aware that while they could voice their concerns during these brief encounters, they had no influence on policy.

Confident in an American Muslim future, Muslims in various suburbs and cities stepped out of the shadows and became more visible. They turned to their own resources and began building mosques and Islamic centers, whose number grew from 598 in 1986 to over 1,250 by 2000. Some of the mosques built in the middle of the century were architecturally non-descript and were remodeled or replaced by new structures with minarets, copulas, and domes, symbols of Islamic architecture. A few of the mosques started social and welfare organizations (such as soup kitchens and free medical clinics) to serve the needy in America, breaking the practices of earlier generations who sent their *zakat* funds to support the poor relatives and the dispossessed of the lands they left behind. Over 200 Islamic schools were established. In the process, Islam was entering the mainstream, and the Muslim community had decided that it was in America to stay. It consciously began to put its imprint on the American landscape, a permanent settlement set in brick, concrete, tile, and stone.

Meanwhile, Arab-American identity had become associated with Christians and secular Muslims from the Arab world. There was a growing consensus among Islamists that Arab identity had been divisive and had led to the disempowerment of the Arabs. From their perspective, any one who identifies himself as Arab, places national over religious identity. Increasingly, Muslim immigrants from Arab nation states identify themselves either as Muslim, or by the citizenship they held prior to emigration: Egyptian, Palestinian, Syrian, and the like. Very rarely does an immigrant identify himself, "I am an Arab Muslim," unless he is from the Gulf area or is trying to make a linguistic or geographical distinction. For many among the third wave immigrants, "Arab" has become a secondary modifier of identity, which is in a state of flux depending on context. Their primary identity can be Shi'i, Muslim, Lebanese, Arab, or American, depending on the circumstances that demand differentiation.

Whereas early mosque activities centered on fostering a social community that shared a common faith, in the 1990s the mosque became a center for creating an Islamic ethnicity based not only on a shared faith, but also on a shared worldview that envisioned a Muslim community engaged with American society, taking its place in the American religious mosaic.

Claiming Muslim Space in America's Pluralism

Who is a Muslim? When does one cease to be a Muslim? What is the relation of Islam to culture, to politics, to economic practices; and how does a Muslim maintain adherence to Islamically prescribed and proscribed admonitions that relate to these issues? Given the broad range of backgrounds and associations, what practices and beliefs are negotiable, fixed, or malleable? How does the cultural baggage carried by the immigrants influence their perception of Islamic culture as it takes root in America? Is there a possibility of reinterpreting Islamic jurisprudence to provide more options for behavior in the American context? Does the slogan "Islam is valid for all times and places" necessitate consensus on a particular prototype that has to be implemented wherever Islam is transplanted, or is there room for reinterpretation to help Muslims adjust to the new environment in which they find themselves? Can Muslims tolerate the different choices that members in the community make or should they deem those who veer from the proclaimed laws as beyond the pale? Can a Muslim live in a non-Muslim environment and continue to be considered a believer? These and other questions have been the focus of extensive discussion and debate during the twentieth century.

The immigrants had no experience of being a minority, of living in diaspora, or of creating institutions or organizing religious communities. They had no imams or religious leaders to provide

instruction in the foundations of the faith. In the nations they left behind, religious affairs were the domain of governments. They had to figure out whether their living in a non-Muslim state, or eating the meat sold in its stores owned by non-Muslims was religiously sanctioned. They sought juridical justification for their choices and counsel on what institutional forms to create.

Islamic juridical opinion has addressed these issues in a variety of contexts throughout Islamic history. The legal opinion of the medieval jurists is often quoted to provide validation for modern interpretations. Given the wide range of opinions, the variety of contexts that they addressed over a span of fourteen centuries, it is not surprising that there is no absolute consensus on the issue.[45] In the contemporary era, the voluntary emigration of Muslims to non-Muslim nations has once again raised the issue of the legitimacy of residing in a non-Muslim environment.

The early immigrants had no Islamic leadership and no access to juridical opinion. They were aware of the *fatwas* of Muhammad Abduh, Shaykh al-Azhar of Egypt permitting the consumption of meat slaughtered by People of the Book (Christians and Jews) as well as Muslim collaboration with non-Muslims for the benefit that accrued to the Muslim community.[46] They were also aware of the *fatwa* by Rashid Rida approving residence of Muslims in a non-Muslim environment. Quoting al-Mawardi, a famous medieval jurist, he reported that the Prophet did not proscribe residence in non-Muslim areas, but had actually allowed Muslims to do so if they were accorded the freedom to practice their faith.[47]

[45] Khaled Abou El Fadl, "Striking a Balance: Islamic Legal Discourse on Muslim Minorities," in *Muslims on the Americanization Path?*, ed. Yvonne Yazbeck Haddad and John L. Esposito (New York: Oxford University Press, 2000) 52. For more details on the subject, see: Khaled Abou El Fadl, "Islamic Law and Muslim Minorities: The Jouristic Discourse on Muslim from the Second/Eighth to the Eleventh/Seventeenth Centuries," *Islamic Law and Society* 1, 2 (1994): 140–87.

[46] "Isti'anat al-Muslimin bi'l-Kuffar wa Ahl al-Bid'a wa al-Ahwa'," in Muhammad 'Amara, *al-A'mal al-Kamila li'l-Imam Muhammad 'Abdu: al-Kitabat al-Siyasiyya* (Cairo: al-Mu'assasa al-'Arabiyya li'l-Dirasat wa'l-Nashr, 1972) 708–15.

[47] Abou El Fadl, "Striking a Balance," 52.

As noted earlier, the immigrants who came after the repeal of the Asia Exclusion Act included Muslims who had given up on the nationalist ideology and were influenced by the Islamic vision of a society that is an alternative to Marxism and capitalism, one that is eager to recreate an Islamic order in the world. Many were influenced by the writings of Mawlana Abu al-A'la al-Mawdudi, founder of the Jama'ati Islami of the subcontinent, and Sayyid Qutb, ideologue of the Muslim Brotherhood in Egypt.[48] Mawdudi's ideology was incubated in the struggle for the creation of an Islamic state in Pakistan, while Qutb's ideas were influenced by what he experienced as racism and his exposure to pro-Israeli anti-Arab, anti-Muslim propaganda during his residence in the United States, as well as by his reactions to the socialist-secularist policies of Abdul Nasser. Both Mawdudi and Qutb advocated a sharp bifurcation between Islam and nationalism, between the Muslim *umma* and all other social and political systems, which they designated as *jahiliyya*, a reference to the polytheistic society that obtained in Arabia at the time of the revelation of the Qur'an. For both, the mission of Muslims in the world is to combat un-Islamic orders and not to compromise with them.

Qutb fashioned an ideology of resistance advocating the creation of a vanguard group who would refuse to live under regimes that persecuted Muslims for their beliefs or placed impediments in the way of creating an Islamic state. Mawdudi traveled extensively in the United States and Canada during the 1960s and 1970s warning the recently arrived Muslim immigrants about living in a non-Muslim environment. He later moderated his views and taught that residence in the United States provides the opportunity for delivering the saving message of Islam to America. Another influencial Muslim speaker, Syed Abu al-Hassan Ali Nadvi of India, traveled extensively in the United States and Canada urging Muslims to maintain a separate community. He urged the immigrants to be steadfast in the faith. "You, therefore, are in America not merely as flesh and blood, not simply as Indians, Pakistanis, Egyptians, Syrians. . . . but as Muslims, one community, one brotherhood. You are Ibrahimi and Muhammadi.

[48] Sayyid Qutb, *Milestones* (Indianapolis: American Trust, 1990).

Know yourself. You have not come here to lose your identity and get fitted into this monstrous machine or to fill your bellies like animals."[49] He warned against being blinded by the search for wealth and losing one's distinctive identity. "Should there be the least danger to faith go back to your native land or to any other place where there is the security of faith; go, and take your family, go even if you have to go on foot."[50]

Overseas, interest in the condition of vulnerable Muslim minorities in the world increased during the 1970s and 1980s. M. Ali Kettani, a North African, wrote a book on Muslim minorities, identifying "minorityness" as a condition of powerlessness of the community, regardless of its numerical strength. He feared that this condition may lead Muslims to compromise with those in power and acquiesce to their demands, restricting their freedom to practice the faith. If that occurs, it becomes their incumbent Islamic duty to try to alter their situation. If they are unable to change their circumstances, they have to emigrate to a more congenial environment where they can practice their faith without impediment, or they have to organize and fight back against their oppressors. To emigrate is to emulate the example of the Prophet in search of freedom to practice the faith. It has a profound religious significance, since in this act they are not accommodating oppressive power but continue to work for the establishment of a just society. This emigration has two possible goals: one seeks the return to the place of origin in order to restore it to the true faith; the other is to establish a permanent settlement in an effort to create a new Islamic society. Kettani recommended that immigrant Muslims create residential enclaves and local institutions that support the building of an Islamic community without divisions according to national origin, class, sectarian, or partisan affiliation. The goal is to protect the community from assimilation into the new environment that would lead to its disintegration. It must guard its distinctiveness and maintain Islamic cultural markers. He urged the Muslim community to take control of the education

---

[49] Syed A. Hassan Ali Nadvi, *Muslims in the West: The Message and Mission* (London: Islamic Foundation, 1983) 111.

[50] Ibid., 158.

of their children, to emphasize the use of the Arabic language, wear Islamic dress, and assume Islamic names. From his perspective, the enclave is not a ghetto, but rather a model Muslim community that fosters and promotes the realization of Islamic principles in daily life, hence becoming a witness to the greater society.[51]

The 1980s brought moderation in Islamic zeal as the excesses of the Iranian Revolution became evident. Lecturers from overseas such as Rashid Ghannushi of Tunisia and Hassan Turabi of Sudan addressed large Muslim gatherings in the United States and began to identify the United States as *dar al-da'wa* ("abode of preaching"), *dar al-solh* ("the abode of treaty") or *dar maftuha* ("an open country") ready for the Islamic message. Both urged Muslims to participate in the United States, trusting in the message of Islam. Emphasizing the pluralistic nature of Islam and its amity with Christianity and Judaism, they urged the believers to be good citizens. There was no need for apprehension since there was no evidence of American persecution of Muslims. In fact, Ghannushi told Muslim audiences that they had more freedom in the United States to reflect on, discuss, and propagate their faith than was available in any Muslim nation.

A few small pockets of Muslims persist in believing that the United States is a *kafir* ("infidel") nation. Those advocating such a perspective include the Tablighi Jama'at (Group of Informers), a group that started in India and spread throughout the world.[52] They renounce politics and focus on emulating the life of the Prophet. Another group are the supporters of the Salafi tradition of Saudi Arabia who attempted with little success to recruit Muslims in the United States to their vision. A third group is Hizb al-Tahrir (Liberation Party), which started in Jordan and has

---

[51] Muhammad Ali Kettani, *Muslim Minorities in the World Today* (London: Mansell, 1986) 9–13. For further discussion on the topic see: Y. Haddad, "The Challenge of Muslim Minorityness: The American Experience," in *The Integration of Islam and Hinduism in Western Europe*, ed. W. A. R. Shadid and P. S. van Koningsveld (Kampen: Kok Pharos, 1991), 134–53.

[52] Barbara D. Metcalf, "New Medinas: The Tablighi Jama'at in America and Europe," in *Making Muslim Space in North America and Europe*, ed. Barbara Daly Metcalf (Berkeley: University of California Press, 1996) 110–30.

spread to Europe with enthusiastic supporters among a fringe group of British Muslims and a few students on American campuses. All three groups insist that the Muslim community must maintain itself as an implant in a foreign body to ensure the separateness, difference, and distinction of Islam, as well as protection from the seductiveness of the American culture to the immigrants, converts, and their children.

Other groups such as the Islamic Society of North America (ISNA), Muslim American Society (MAS), and the Islamic Circle of North America (ICNA), who mostly adhere to the teachings of the Muslim Brotherhood of the Arab East and the Jama'ati Islami of the subcontinent, had also started from the conviction that engagement with secular American society is to be avoided. ISNA moderated its stance in 1986 and began advocating participation in American society, albeit on Muslim terms. Both ISNA and ICNA have been engaged in various efforts of interfaith dialogue. ICNA and MAS have lately opened up their conventions to non-Muslim speakers.

The majority of Muslims in the United States (estimated at over 80%) however, are un-mosqued; they have embraced the fact that they are part of American society and operate with little concern for what the compromise might cost. Many look with disdain at organized mosque centers and believe that non-practicing Muslims are on the right path just as those who attend regular mosque services. Thus the challenges for the leadership of Muslim mosque organizations persist: Should they consider un-mosqued Muslims as beyond the pale? Should Muslims strive for uniformity as they struggle to maintain unity and forge one community out of many? What options can be tolerated and still be considered within the scope of normative Islam? What shape should the ideal Muslim community take? Whose interpretation of these issues is authentic and who has the authority to judge its validity?

While the new immigrants and the foreign "experts" were raising questions and debating the legitimacy of living in a non-Muslim state, the handful of imams who were in the United States were assuring their congregations that they have nothing to fear in the American context, since the United States is committed to democracy and religious freedom, hence promising Muslims a great future free from the supervision of autocratic regimes. Mohammad Abdul-Rauf, imam of the Islamic Center of Washington, D.C., warned against undue apprehension about the ability of Muslims to maintain the imperatives of Islamic life and practice in the United States. He considered efforts to create Islamic enclaves as unnecessary because of the promise of "the hospitable American melting pot" to make room for Muslims to create their own institutions and interpret their own faith in line with Islamic principles. He called on Muslims to look at the history of Islam and its tenacity and ability to withstand the cultural onslaught of fourteen centuries of alien cultures. America, he believed, makes room for Muslims, "not only to survive but also to flourish in honor and dignity."[53]

Others, spurred in part by the immigration of committed Muslims and by the intensifying anti-Muslim, anti-Arab atmosphere in the United States reformulated their Arab-American identity and grounded it in Islam. One was Muhammad T. Mehdi (from Iraq), who first organized the Federation of Associations of Arab-American Relations to educate the American public and Congress about issues in the Middle East and then the Action Committee on Arab-American Relations. An advocate of the American values of justice, freedom, and democracy, he became disillusioned with the effectiveness of Arab identity when the United States did not deliver on its promise of self-determination to the Palestinians.[54] He considered the creation of the state of Israel at the expense of the Palestinian people to be unjust. Mehdi later attempted to galvanize the diverse Muslim community to join him in reaching out to other Americans, expecting that the growing Muslim population from all over the world could provide additional popular support for his causes. Believing in the essential

---

[53] Muhammad Abdul-Rauf, "The Future of the Islamic Tradition in North America," in *The Muslim Community in North America*, ed. Earle H. Waugh, et al. (Edmonton: University of Alberta Press, 1983) 271–72.

[54] Mohammad T. Mehdi, *Of Lions Chained: An Arab Looks at America* (San Francisco: New World Press, [1962]).

goodness of the American people, he was convinced that if they became aware of the injustices perpetrated against the Palestinians, financed and supported by the American taxpayers, American policy would change.[55] In his Islamic phase, he established the National Council of Islamic Affairs, an Islamic action committee that encouraged Muslims to run for office. (He set an example by running for a senate seat in New York where he received 86,000 votes.) He accused the United States of being silent about Israeli policies of "anti-gentilism" that discriminate against its Christian and Muslim population. He worked hard to incorporate Muslims into the American public square through networking, lobbying, and publishing pamphlets and books in support of his causes. He was extremely proud to see, after great effort, the crescent and star (as a symbol of Islam) displayed on the Ellipse in Washington next to the Christmas tree and the Menorah.[56]

For Ismail al-Faruqi,[57] a Palestinian, the journey to Islamic identity unfolded in the American academy. With graduate degrees from Harvard and the University of Indiana, and post-doctoral studies at Al-Azhar University in Cairo, he began his career as a university professor. During the first phase of his intellectual journey, he believed in the power of Arabism as a culture and civilization to create a universal ethical system by promoting standards in human relations as enjoined in the Qur'an. For him, Arabism is not Arab nationalism or ethno-centrism, which developed under colonial rule, but an all-inclusive identity that is infused with Islamic values. It is not rooted in European ideologies of nationalism; rather, it is grounded in the Arabic Qur'an and shared by all Muslims whose culture, values, and ethos are inspired by its revelation.[58]

---

[55] Mohammad T. Mehdi, *Terrorism: Why America is the Target* (New York: New World Press, 1988).

[56] Mohammad T. Mehdi, *Peace in Palestine* (New York: New World Press, 1976).

[57] See John L. Esposito, "Ismail R. Al-Faruqi: Muslim Scholar-Activist," in *The Muslims of America*, ed. Yvonne Yazbeck Haddad (New York: Oxford University Press, 1991) 65–79.

[58] For his ideas on Arabism, see: Ismail Raji al-Faruqi, *On Arabism: Urubah and Religion* (Amsterdam: Djambatan, 1962).

By the early 1970s, al-Faruqi began to share the general Arab disenchantment with Arab identity and turned to Islam. Reflecting on this period of his life, he reminisced, "There was a time in my life [. . .] when all I cared about was proving to myself that I could win my physical and intellectual existence from the West. But, when I won it, it became meaningless. I asked myself: Who am I? A Palestinian, a philosopher, a liberal humanist? My answer was: I am a Muslim."[59] From then on, he promoted Islam as the only umbrella ideology that can bring Muslims together. He criticized nationalism as an instrument used by the west to divide. Purified from its accretions and its compromises with western colonialism, authentic Islam can bring about the revitalization of Muslim societies. In the process, Muslims need to avoid economic and political dependency, social and cultural emulation of the west, political fragmentation and military impotence. The goal is to liberate Jerusalem and restore it to Muslim control.[60]

He became especially interested in the potential creation of a worldwide Muslim leadership in the United States. Besides mentoring large numbers of international graduate students at Temple University, he helped organize intellectual institutions dedicated to the task of "Islamizing knowledge." He argued that all knowledge is grounded in value systems. He believed that infusing the social sciences and the humanities with an Islamic foundation would help bring about the revival of Islam in the modern world. Towards this goal, he helped establish the American Association of Muslim Social Scientists, the International Institute of Islamic Thought in Northern Virginia, and the Islamic College in Chicago to provide committed Islamic leadership, not only for the immigrant community, but more importantly, to the whole world of Islam. His writings were popular among a significant segment of Muslim students on American campuses who found in them the way to maintain a distinctive identity that enhanced their strategy of survival in a hostile environment. Al-Faruqi recommended the

---

[59] As quoted in M. Tareq Quraishi, *Ismail al-Faruqi: An Enduring Legacy* (Plainfield, IN: The Muslim Student Association, 1987) ii.

[60] Ismail Raji al-Faruqi, *Tawhid: Its Implications for Thought and Life* (Kuala Lumpur: The International Institute of Islamic Thought, 1982).

appropriation of an Islamic ideology that emphasized that Muslims were not beggars in the United States, but active participants in the building of a just society. The adoption of an Islamic ideology was promoted as a mechanism to free the immigrant from the sense of guilt for achieving some measure of success in the United States.

At the same time, al-Faruqi sought to carve a space for Islam in the American religious mosaic by attempting to integrate Islam. He found the definition of America as a Judeo-Christian nation quite exclusionary, keeping the Muslims outside the bounds of being fully recognized and celebrated citizens of the United States. He participated in interfaith dialogue with the World Council of Churches in Geneva[61] as well as various groups in the United States, to promote the idea of dialogue among the "Abrahamic faiths." He emphasized that Judaism, Christianity, and Islam are grounded in the same source of faith, the God of Abraham.[62] He also sought to integrate Islam as a subject of study in the American Academy of Religion by forming the Islamic Studies Section, which provided a venue for scholars to discuss Islam as a living faith in the United States and not as an alien "Oriental" religion.

Al-Faruqi also sought to construct a modern universal Islamic culture that is not only relevant, but also appealing in the American environment. He co-authored a book celebrating Muslim cultural achievement.[63] He disagreed with the sentiment among some immigrants that called for austerity and piety, banning music and art, and urged Muslims to surround themselves with Islamic decorations and artifacts in their homes and to participate in Islamic events such as *eid* celebrations. He believed that Muslims in the United States should adopt the practice prevalent among African-American Muslims and make the mosque a family-centered place, where women attended and participated in

61 *Christian Mission and Islamic Da'wah: Proceedings of the Chambesy Dialogue Consultation* (Leister: The Islamic Foundation, 1982).

62 Ismail Raji al-Faruqi, *Trialogue of the Abrahamic Faiths* (Herndon, VA: International Institute of Islamic Thought, 1982).

63 Ismail Raji al-Faruqi, *Islam and Culture* (Kuala Lumpur: ABIM, 1980).

mosque services. The mosque, he believed, should not only be the center for maintaining people in the faith, but also, and more importantly, should be crucial in fashioning the Muslim family, the most important social unit for the preservation of Islam in American society. Asked if he wanted to create a reformed Islam for North America, similar to Reformed Judaism, he replied, "No, my model is Conservative Judaism."[64]

By the middle of the 1980s, the Muslim immigrants who came in the post-1965 period stopped debating whether they could live in the United States and maintain their faith, or should leave to live under the jurisdiction of an Islamic state. Rather the discussion shifted to the definition of Muslim life in the American context—the institutions necessary for the maintenance of Muslim identity, and the scope of Muslim participation in the American public square. The debate among those in the community committed to practicing the faith in America centered on which model was to be emulated. The choice appeared to be between the Mennonite and the Jewish options. The Mennonites, despite their particular social, economic, cultural, and political outlook on life, were able to maintain their faith unchanged in the context of a secular state. The Jewish option was more appealing. They represented a non-Christian religion whose approximately six million adherents had gained recognition as equal participants in fashioning the American society. Not only did American leaders talk about America as a Judeo-Christian country, but Jewish leadership was represented in the centers of power: in government, in the academy, and in all aspect of society. The Muslims wanted a similar place.

In 1993, a new organization came into existence, the North American Association of Muslim Professionals and Scholars (NAAMPS). At its inaugural meeting, Fathi Osman, an internationally recognized Islamic scholar who had for many years edited the London journal *Arabia*, spoke with confidence about the Muslim future in America. He envisioned a new role for Muslims, one grounded not in fear or isolation, but in engagement with the society; not in retrenchment, but in exploration of new ways of

---

[64] Conversation with the author in 1982.

leadership and participation. He saw the United States as an open venue for the development of new ideas and new visions. He challenged the Muslims of America blessed with this freedom to lead the revival of Islam in the world. He described the Muslims of the Arab world as ossified; they study Islam of the past, while the Muslims of the United States have the capacity to be the pioneers of a new interpretation that will help solve the problems Muslims face. They can envision new and unlimited possibilities and help bring about a brighter future.[65]

Other speakers at the conference included Maher Hathout, President of the Islamic Center of Southern California, who called on Muslims to engage in realistic assessments of their problems and cease being fixated on the defense of Islam against its detractors. He reminded the community that the boundaries of isolation have not all been created by the suspicions of the larger society about Muslims, but that they were, in many cases, self-imposed out of fear. He urged the audience to reject separation and counseled reaching out to the larger community, to try and understand the American society. The first step in such an endeavor is to learn to listen, to alter the fixation with the rhetorical apologetic that Muslims have engaged in as a defense of Islam. He also counseled Muslims to engage in a more realistic and practical assessment of their condition rather than talk exclusively about ideals. Finally, he assured them that regardless of their efforts, their children were on the path of becoming American. "While we huddle together as Pakistanis or Egyptians or Iranians or whatever else, our children are, whether we believe it or like it or hate it or not, American kids. The question should be whether they will be Muslim-American kids or just American kids. Any one who believes that he will raise an Egyptian boy in America is wrong: the maximum we can do is have a distorted Egyptian kid. The grandchildren will be without doubt American."[66]

---

65 Mohammad Fathi Osman, "Towards a Vision and an Agenda for the Future of Muslim Ummah," in *Islam: A Contemporary Perspective*, ed. Muhammad Ahmadullah Siddiqui (Chicago: NAAMPS, 1994) 13–22.

66 Maher Hathout, "Islamic Work in North America: Challenges and Opportunities," in *Islam*, ed. Siddiqui, 13.

A third speaker, Salam Al-Marayati, also urged the audience to engage with America and take advantage of its freedom. He noted that his political activities on behalf of Muslims overseas were probably more effective than the combined effort of all the members of the Organization of the Islamic Conference. He urged Muslims to carve an "independent pathway." The choice is not between isolation and assimilation, but must be engagement with the society, taking America at its promise and working within the system to breach the walls of "the other."[67] "What good is our message, if we cannot deliver it to the world, to the humanity, or to the public? Contrarily, we cannot assimilate and lose our Islamic identity because we want to be involved in some ethnic group, or we think that is the American thing to do. [. . .] Yes, we must be Muslims, offer Islamic values, and be American citizens all in one."[68]

The Aftermath of 9/11

While scholars have been studying the immigration and integration of Arabs and Muslims in the United States and comparing their adjustment to that of other initially ostracized religious groups such as Catholics and Jews, in the aftermath of 9/11, it may be necessary to compare the treatment of Arabs and Muslims with that of the Germans during World War I, the Japanese during World War II, and the Jews during the Cold War. The policies adopted by the Bush administration are reminiscent of measures adopted during these critical moments in American history that suspended American legal protection of all citizens and targeted those identified as a threat to the nation.

The last wave of Muslim immigrants had consciously and deliberately stepped out of the isolation that the immigrants of the 1960s and 1970s had maintained because they feared for the survival of Islam. Muslims embarked in the 1990s on a policy of engagement with American society that culminated in joining

[67] Salam al-Marayati, "Formulating an Agenda of Political Actions for North American Muslims," in *Islam*, ed. Siddiqui, 64–69.
[68] Ibid., 70.

Arab organizations and publicly supporting the Bush-Cheney ticket in the 2000 presidential election. The impetus for the endorsement was the fact that Bush met with the leadership of Arab and Muslim organizations and listened to their concerns, while Gore ignored them. Furthermore, during the presidential debates, Bush questioned the fairness of the profiling of Arabs and Muslims. Upon taking office, however, the Bush administration shied away from engaging with the Muslim community. This policy changed after 9/11 when President Bush visited the Islamic Center in Washington, D.C., and in an effort to calm public anger, but to the consternation of many of his supporters, declared Islam a "religion of peace." The government now sought engagement with the community for a price.

The attacks of 9/11 appear to have settled the internal debate that was taking place among policymakers in the United States. With the collapse of the Soviet Union, a growing number of political and religious officials had been casting around for a new enemy. Some found it convenient to designate "fundamentalist Islam" as the imminent threat, "the other" that needed to be eliminated. Several Israeli leaders had for several decades been identifying Islam as the "enemy." The attacks of 9/11 revealed a growing consensus among many of the Beltway pundits and the press that Israel and America are co-victims of Islamic hatred of Judaism and Christianity.

Also subscribing to this view were members of the fundamentalist Christian community. Their theologians had interpreted the signs of the end times after the Israeli victory of 1967 to include a major battle between Jews restored to Israel and the Muslims. The battle would herald the imminent return of the Messiah. They welcomed the intensification of conflict between the two faiths since it would mean the final redemption of the Jews. Their ministers engaged in demonizing Islam and its Prophet with gusto reminiscent of the discourse that launched the Crusades and justified European colonization of Muslim nations.

The initial impact of 9/11 on the Muslim community was one of deep shock and fear of potential backlash. Muslims were subsequently surprised and pleased by the response of some in the

Christian and Jewish community who supported them. They were grateful to the rabbis and ministers who volunteered to stand guard at mosques, schools, bookstores, and other Islamic institutions to keep avengers away. They were amazed at the number of American women who donned scarves for a day in solidarity with Muslim women who veil. They were also touched by the little gestures of kindness, of neighbors who offered to act as escorts or purchase groceries. They were pleased that Americans were finally interested in Islam and were reading about the religion and getting acquainted with the tenets of their faith.

For Muslims, the most distressing measure adopted by the government in response to 9/11 is HR3162, commonly known as USA PATRIOT (Providing Appropriate Tools Required to Intercept and Obstruct Terrorism) Act of October 24, 2001, which has in essence lifted all legal protection of liberty for Muslims and Arabs in the United States. It sanctions the monitoring of individuals, organizations, and institutions without notification. Its provisions have been protested by the American Bar Association, the American Librarians Association, and the American Civil Liberties Union. Several Arab and Muslim organizations have recently sued the American government insisting that this act is un-American. Former Congresswoman, Mary Rose Oakar, President of the American-Arab Anti-Discrimination Committee said that it was "completely incompatible with basic civil liberties, most notably freedom from unreasonable search and seizure by the government guaranteed by the Fourth Amendment to the Constitution."[69]

Meanwhile, the identification of a terrorist in the United States had slowly mutated from "Arab" to "Muslim." The critical transfer became embedded in American law when Congress passed HR 1710, the Comprehensive Anti-terrorism Act of 1995 after the Oklahoma City bombing. The bill sanctioned, among

---

[69] Other Arab-American and Islamic organizations that joined ADC in the brief include: Muslim Community Association of Ann Arbor, Arab Community Center for Economic and Social Services, Bridge Refugee and Sponsorship Services, Council on American and Islamic Relations, Islamic Center of Portland and Masjid as-Sabir of Portland, OR.

other security measures, airport profiling of potential terrorists. The profile was not of a Timothy McVeigh, but of an Arab or a Muslim. Arabs and Muslims are concerned that, while the Anti-Terrorism Act had sanctioned the incarceration of Arabs and Muslims with secret evidence, the Patriot Act has sanctioned their incarceration with no evidence.

They have also been greatly distressed by the security measures adopted by the Bush Administration, which were perceived as anti-Muslim, rather than anti-terrorism. The measures include a declared war on a Muslim definition of the role of women in society. The American government has set up a bureaucracy in the Department of State specifically engaged in liberating the women of Islam. The question is whether this liberation is from Islam and its values. Textbooks in Muslim countries are being monitored by United States embassies for anti-western, anti-American, or anti-Israeli content. It appears to many that the only "Islam" that can be taught is one approved by the CIA. Other measures include the monitoring of NGOs, civic, charitable, and religious organizations. Out of fear of transfer of funds to terrorist organizations, the American government has in effect assumed a veto power over one of the basic tenets of the Islamic faith by monitoring charities and organizations that support orphans and widows overseas.

Equally troubling were the raids on the homes and offices of the national Muslim leadership in northern Virginia by several federal agencies. Muslims perceived this action as a sign that the United States government was now looking for a new leadership. This seemed surprising since this leadership had been criticized by Muslims precisely because it was cooperating with the American government. The raids raised questions about what kind of Islam would America now tolerate. A few individuals have stepped up and volunteered to lead the Muslims into "moderation." Several have been supported and funded by various agencies of the United States government. Their mission is to provide new reflections and interpretations of Islam. They have opened offices and are in the process of leading others into "right thinking." To date, they appear to have a few followers since they are perceived as agents of the effort to undermine Islam.

Other profound changes appear underway; their ramifications are still unfolding. For the majority of Muslims, who emigrated with the idea that if things did not work out they could always return home, the attacks appear to have settled the "Myth of Return": Muslims are here to stay. The question for them is how to adjust to the intensified scrutiny by anti-immigration groups and government security agencies that demand repeated public demonstrations of patriotism and allegiance to America and its policies. Many had a hard time convincing their fellow Americans that because America had been attacked, they felt attacked, too. Their repeated denunciations of terrorism as un-Islamic did not seem to be sufficient. Some offered to act as a bridge linking the United States government with Muslim organizations overseas and governments in heavily Muslim countries. Others volunteered to serve in the armed services. Thousands volunteered to act as translators, though few were hired due to heightened suspicion of their ethnicity and/or religious affiliation.

That the whole community is under scrutiny has brought about other changes. There is little room for public conflict. There is a new relationship between the mosqued and un-mosqued, who had previously disagreed on issues pertaining to integration and assimilation. In the domestic reaction that followed 9/11, exemplified in the policies adopted by the government and the tone assumed by some of the press and some of the evangelical clergy, both groups were targets of hate, of discrimination and profiling regardless of their religious or political adherence. Sermons in mosques have been restricted to devotional topics. Islamic literature that used to be available for free distribution has disappeared from most public places. Self-censorship has also extended to websites and recommended links.

Another noticeable change is the prominence of Muslim women in the public square. While a few, feeling threatened by a feeling of insecurity and vulnerability, took off the veil to avoid attacks, many put it on. As men began to keep a low profile, the women took charge. Many Muslim women began to assume important positions in the administration of Islamic institutions, as spokespersons and defenders of the community. In this period of tribulation, rather than being delegated to the "sisters" committee, designated as "parallel but equal," men and women are "together and equal." They raised funds for the victims of 9/11 and coordinated blood drives for the wounded. They also marched to protest discrimination against Muslims. At the same time, concern over government policy of incarcerating or deporting males for infractions of the laws has placed some women under duress. They are reluctant to report domestic problems in order to safeguard their husbands' and their children's future.

Also noticeable is the fact that the community has embarked on coalition building with human rights, religious rights, and civil rights groups. Relating to non-Muslims has become a priority. They have promoted interfaith occasions, inviting churches and synagogues to come and visit the mosques and engage in dialogue. They have joined national organizations that are seeking justice against corporations and sweatshops, protection of the environment, and peaceful resolution of conflicts. They have begun to seek to build coalitions with civil liberties organizations. Sill, many feel that because of their ethnicity or religious affiliation they no longer have the luxury to disagree with government policy. While freedom of thought is a right for all Americans, there seems to be an exception if the Americans are Arab or Muslim. The policy of "You are either with us or against us" appears to have no room for an independent interpretation of what it means to be Muslim.

Conclusion

For over a century, immigrants from the Arab world have prospered in the United States. They have "made it" by working hard, carefully shedding their particular cultural distinctions, compromising, and blending in. They have not, as yet, been welcomed as a group into the American mainstream. The Christians among them who have achieved leadership positions, even as elected governors and senators, mostly abandoned Eastern Christianity, whether Orthodox, Melkite, or Maronite and joined mainline American churches. Many Muslims question whether the price of belonging in America is contingent on the renunciation of Islam. They are still waiting to be accepted on their own terms into the American definition of its constituent faith communities.

From the outset, officials in various agencies of the American government raised questions about their fitness to qualify for citizenship in America based on issues of race and color[70] Spooked by the influx of large groups of immigrants (predominantly from southern and eastern Europe) during the first two decades of the twentieth century, the American public appeared less inclined to welcome Middle Easterners. Helen Hattab Samhan, Deputy Director of the Arab American Institute, noted that "A judge in South Carolina ruled Lebanese immigrants even though they may look white, they are not that particular free white person" designated by the 1790 Act of Congress and hence not worthy of citizenship.[71] After a decade of legal debates, the American courts ruled that they qualified as white and were therefore able to become citizens.

In the post-World War II period, when the United States was reinventing itself as a pluralistic society, immigrants from the Arab world found themselves publicly and deliberately excluded from the mainstream of American politics. Helen Hatab Samhan wrote about their experience, "In the present period, anti-Arab attitudes and behavior have their roots, not in the traditional motives of structurally excluding a group perceived as inferior, but in politics." She indicated that the political nature of this racism was rooted in the Arab-Israeli conflict since those who supported the Palestinian cause were subjected to this exclusion whether or not they were Arab-Americans.[72] "It has been not so much Arab origin as Arab political activity in America that has engendered a

[70] 213 Fed. 812 (District Court, E.D. South Carolina, 1914), at 357 as cited by Moore, *al-Mughtaribun*, 53; Khalil A. Bishara, *Origin of the Modern Syrian*. Cited in Michael Suleiman, "Early Arab-Americans: The Search for Identity," in *Crossing the Waters, Arabic-Speaking Immigrants to the United States before 1940*, ed. Eric J. Hoogland (Washington, D.C.: Smithsonian Institution Press, 1987) 44.

[71] Helen Hatab Samhan, "Politics and Exclusion: The Arab American Experience," *Journal of Palestine Studies* 16.2 (1987) 14.

[72] Ibid., 11–28.

new form of 'political' racism that takes prejudice and exclusion out of the arena of personal relations into the arena of public information and public policy."[73] This political exclusion was propagated by their political rivals, the American Jewish organization who tagged Arab-American activists as an "artificial constituency," a sort of illegitimate group of foreign agents undermining Israel.[74] This eventually brought a variety of government agencies including the CIA, INS, FBI, IRS, the Department of State and the United States Customs Service, to coordinate monitoring the Arab-American community in an effort to ferret out terrorists and intimidate the community, weakening its effectiveness, and scaring off its allies and sympathizers.[75] Not one instance of violation of United States laws was uncovered.[76] "In the situation of Arab Americans today, exclusion from ethnic politics (i.e., acting as a constituency) is not so much by ignorance or prejudice as by political design. And because Jewish Americans are their main 'adversaries' and can recall their own past victimization (anti-Semitism), the Arab Americans *in their exclusion* often emerge as the villains."[77]

The 1990s witnessed an increase in hostility towards Arabs and Muslims in the Untied States. The hostile atmosphere appears to have been encouraged by several interests. They include the conservative wing of the Republican Party, the religious right, the pro-Israel lobby, and leaders of autocratic Arab states. Events overseas precipitated measures that led to racial profiling and targeting of Arabs and Muslims, along with a growing atmosphere of hostility towards Islam. An act of Congress, a decision of the Supreme Court, and a Presidential executive order legitimated the incarceration of Arabs and/or Muslims using secret evidence. In a sense, they were treated as different from other citizens of the United States since they were denied the basic presumption of innocence until proven guilty. Thus, at the

73 Ibid., 16.
74 Amy K. Groot and Steven J. Rosen, eds. *The Campaign to Discredit Israel* (Washington, D.C.: American Israel Public Affairs Committee, 1983) 3–12.
75 Fischbach, "Government Pressures," 89.
76 *The New York Times*, May 25, 1973.
77 Samhan, "Politics and Exclusion," 26.

beginning of the twenty-first century, the United States, once again, seemed to be questioning whether the members of one group have the same rights as other citizens. This time the discrimination was based not on color, or political affiliation, rather on the perennial fear of the Saracen and the commitment to an Islamic ideology.

Since the 1870s, immigrants from the Arab world to the United States have been engaged in the dialectical process of being and becoming American.[78] This process has been protracted, painful, and exacerbated by the new war on terrorism. Each immigrant wave brought its distinctive identity, shaped by events over which it had no control, and fashioned by its generation as a response to prevailing conditions and to expectations set up by the government of the respective country from which it came. These identities have also been directly impacted by the vagaries of America's interests, policies, and actions and inactions in the Middle East, as well as the prevailing prejudice towards Arabs and Muslims. Once here, immigrants encounter an America that appears open for a redefinition of its own identity to accommodate the participation of its new citizens, but they experience it as racist and unreceptive to their concerns. America is experienced as having a fluid definition of itself, but at the same time, unwilling to allow the immigrants space to express their equal humanity.

There appears to be a growing tendency in the American media to portray Arabs and Muslims as the consummate "other," as terrorists, or, more recently, as the enemy of all cherished Western values.[79] At the same time, some Arabs, surveying the history and experience of the Muslim community worldwide, see themselves as the victims of a virulent anti-Muslim hatred that

---

[78] Areas designated as the Arab world by the State Department include the Middle East and North Africa.

[79] Hamid Mawlana, George Gerbner and Herbert I. Schiller eds., *Triumph of the Image: The Media's War in the Persian Gulf–A Global Perspective* (Boulder, CO: Westview, 1992); Nicholas Berry, *Foreign Policy and the Press: An Analysis of the New York Times' Coverage of U.S. Foreign Policy* (New York: Greenwood Press, 1990); Kenneth I. Vaux, *Ethics and the Gulf War: Religion, Rhetoric, and Righteousness* (Boulder, CO: Westview, 1992).

seeks to subjugate them. They trace this victimization from the Crusades and the *Reconquista*, through the age of imperialism, and see it reinforced in contemporary events. Currently, two important factors continue to fashion their identity as they attempt to fit and feel comfortable in the United States: the perception of Arabs and the Arab community in the United States as victims of American and Israeli interests; and the sense that the American environment is not only biased against them, but infused with an endemic prejudice that has been perpetuated in literature,[80] the media,[81] and the movies.[82]

Several events in the late twentieth century appear to have had a profound impact on the formulation of Arab-American and Muslim identity in the United States. Events that heightened Americans' negative perceptions of Arabs, Islam, and Muslims include: the Israeli preemptive strike on Egypt, Syria, and Jordan in 1967, the oil boycott of 1973, the Islamic Revolution in Iran in 1979, the Rushdie Affair of 1989, and the Gulf Wars. The 1967 war provided the impetus for the formation of the American-Arab organizations that sought to ameliorate the negative image of Arabs in America, to provide a venue for airing their frustration, and to give accurate information. They attempted to redress what they perceived to be the one-sided reports about the Arab and Muslim world and sought to exercise their political rights to have an input into the shaping of policy. The American reaction to the

[80] Reeva S. Simon, *The Middle East in Crime Fiction: Mysteries, Spy Novels, and Thrillers from 1916 to the 1980s* (New York: Lilian Barber Press, 1989); Albert Hourani, *Western Attitudes Towards Islam* (Southampton: University of Southampton, 1974).

[81] Linda Steet, *Veils and Daggers: A Century of National Geographic's Representation of the Arab World* (Philadelphia: Temple University, 2000); Edmund Ghareeb, *Split Vision: The Portrayal of Arabs in the American Media* (Washington, D.C.: American-Arab Affairs Council, 1983); Janice J. Terry, *Mistaken Identity: Arab Stereotypes in Popular Writing* (Washington, D.C.: Arab-American Affairs Council, 1985).

[82] Jack G. Shaheen, *Arab and Muslim Stereotyping in American Popular Culture* (Washington, D.C.: Center for Muslim Christian Understanding, 1997); idem, *Reel Bad Arabs: How Hollywood Vilifies a People* (New York: Olive Branch Press, 2001); idem, *The TV Arab* (Bowling Green, OH: The Popular Press, 1984).

Islamic Revolution in Iran and the anti-Muslim sentiments gen-erated in the American media with headlines such as "America Held Hostage" focused Muslim attention on the unforgiving and sustained rejection of political Islam. It raised questions about American support for Israel, which defines itself as a Jewish state, and the American rejection of Muslim attempts to create Islamic states.

The Gulf Wars brought to the fore a new generation of Arab and Muslim activists seeking to change American policies by operating within the system. The majority did not approve of either American wars on Iraq, not because they were fond of Saddam Hussein or his policies; rather, they were not convinced by the justification of the government for launching the attacks. They were concerned that the United States government did not give diplomacy a chance, since from their perspective, it was bent on destroying Iraq's army in order to maintain Israeli domination of the Arab world.

Unlike the activists of the 1970s, the newest generation of Arab-Americans is not spending time on establishing umbrella organizations, writing constitutions for these organizations, or running elections for officials or spokespersons. Rather, it has adopted modern means of communication including the internet to create networks committed to justice and peace. These recent Arab-Americans collaborate with existing organizations for human rights, minority rights, and religious rights. These activists are mostly in their twenties and thirties, and they take American values very seriously. They believe that they are working to create a better America, one that is not blinded by special interests but is truly guided by the values it preaches. In the process, they believe that they are truly Arab—truly American.

There is a marked difference between those who emigrated in the 1960s and the children and grandchildren of the immigrants of the 1870s. The latter have moved into the middle class and identify as Americans. They and their relatives have been drafted into the American military forces and have served their country with distinction. One recently boasted that he had "three times as many relatives [three nephews] serving in the American military, defending American freedom in Iraq as the whole Congress of the United States put together."

The new immigrants who came as adults in the 1960s with preformed identities and a distinctive worldview are in the process of negotiating their identity in a hostile American environment. Increasingly their children are reshaping them into Americans. For the children, America is the only homeland they know. They often repeat, "I want my parents' religion but not their culture." The parents, on the other hand, have been teaching their Arab culture as Islam, and they want to keep their children within the tradition. It is too early to guess where this process will lead, especially in light of American hostility to non-privatized Islam. Increasingly, Americans are asking them to define themselves vis-à-vis America. What does it mean to them to be an American? Do they want to be an American or a hyphenated-American? Do they think of themselves as Muslims living in America? Do they think of themselves as American Muslims? Or do they think of themselves as Americans who happen to be Muslim? While the answers to such questions may vary, there is no doubt that the American public, the American security apparatus, and the American government are increasingly demanding a clear and unequivocal answer. In the process, many young people who grew up identifying themselves as American and Muslim are increasingly experiencing relentless prejudice and discrimination. Some have become aware that, as one woman put it, although "I feel American, I bleed American, my country denies me that identity because I am a Muslim." Tempered by prevalent hatred and "othering" many are reidentifying themselves as Arab-American or Muslim-American.

Works Cited

Abdu, Muhammad. "Isti'anat al- Muslimin bi'l-Kuffar wa Ahl al-Bid'a wa al-Ahwa'." In *al-A'mal al-Kamila li'l-Imam Muhammad 'Abdu: al-Kitabat al-Siyasiyya*. Ed. Muhammad 'Amara. Cairo: al-Mu'assasa al-'Arabiyya li'l-Dirasat wa'l-Nashr, 1972.

Abdul-Rauf, Muhammad. "The Future of the Islamic Tradition in North America." In *The Muslim Community in North America*. Ed. Earle H. Waugh, et al. Edmonton: University of Alberta Press, 1983.

Abou El Fadl, Khaled. "Islamic Law and Muslim Minorities: The Juristic Discourse on Muslim From the Second/Eighth to the Eleventh/Seventeenth Centuries." *Islamic Law and Society* 1 (1994): 140–87.

———. "Striking a Balance: Islamic Legal Discourse on Muslim Minorities." In *Muslims on the Americanization Path?* Ed. Yvonne Yazbeck Haddad and John Le Esposito. New York: Oxford University Press, 2000.

Abraham, Nabeel. "Detroit's Yemeni Workers." *MERIP Reports* 53 (1977): 3–9.

———. "National and Local Politics: A Study of Political Conflict in the Yemeni Immigrant Community of Detroit, Michigan." Diss., University of Michigan, 1978.

Ahmed, K., Arne Rudvin, et al. *Christian Mission and Islamic Da'wah: Proceedings of the Chambesy Dialogue Consultation* (Leister: The Islamic Foundation, 1982).

al-Faruqi, Ismail Raji. *Islam and Culture*. Kuala Lumpur: ABIM, 1980.

———. *On Arabism: Urubah and Religion*. Amsterdam: Djambatan, 1962.

———. *Tawhid: Its Implications for Thought and Life*. Kuala Lumpur: The International Institute of Islamic Thought, 1982.

———. *Trialogue of the Abrahamic Faiths*. Herndon, VA: International Institute of Islamic Thought, 1986.

al-Marayati, Salam. "Formulating an Agenda of Political Actions for North American Muslims." In Siddiqui.

al-Qazzaz, Ayad. "Images of the Arabs in American Social Science Textbooks." In *Arabs in America: Myths and Realities.* Ed. Baha Abu Laban and Faith T. Ziadeh. Willmette, IL: Medina University Press International, 1975.

al-Qazzaz, Ayad. "The Arab Lobby: Toward an Arab-American Political Identity." *al-Jadid* 3, no. 14 (1997).

'Amara, Muhammad, *al'A'mal al-Kamila li'l-Imam Muhammad 'Abdu: al-Kitabat al-Siyasiyya* (Cairo: al-Mu'assasa al-'Arabiyya li'l-Dirasat wa'l-Nashr, 1972).

Arab American Institute. "Demographics" [online]. Washington, D.C.: Arab American Institute, 2003. [cited 5/13/2003] Available at *http://www.aaiusa.org/demographics.htm#Religion3.*

Aswad, Barbara. *Arabic-Speaking Communities in American Cities.* New York: Center for Migration Studies, 1984.

Bakst, Jerome. "Arabvertising: The New Brand of Arab Propaganda." *Times of Israel*, April 1975: 15–23.

Bassiouni, M. C., ed. "The Civil Rights of Arab-Americans: 'The Special Measures.'" Information Paper 10. Belmont, MA: Association of Arab-American University Graduates, 1974.

Berman, Jerry. "A Public Policy Report." Washington, D.C.: ACLU, October 10, 1982.

Berry, Nicholas. *Foreign Policy and the Press: An Analysis of The New York Times' Coverage of U.S. Foreign Policy.* New York: Greenwood Press, 1990.

Dahbany-Miraglia, Dina. "American Yemenite Jewish Inter-ethnic Strategies." In *Persistence and Flexibility: Anthropological Perspectives on the American Jewish Experience.* Ed. Walter B. Zenner. Albany: State University of New York Press, 1988.

Daniel, Norman. *Islam and the West: The Making of an Image.* Oxford: One World, 1993.

Elkholy, Abdo A. *The Arab Moslems in the United States: Religion and Assimilation.* New Haven: College and University Press, 1966.

Esposito, John. "Ismail R. Al-Faruqi: Muslim Scholar-Activist." In *The Muslims of America.* Ed. Yvonne Yazbeck Haddad. New York: Oxford University Press, 1991.

Findley, Paul. *They Dare Speak Out: People and Institutions Confront Israel's Lobby*. Chicago: Lawrence Hill Books, 1989.

Fischbach, Michael R. "Government Pressure against Arabs in the United States." *Journal of Palestine Studies* 14.3 (1985): 87–100.

Gerbner, George, et al, eds. *Triumph of the Image: The Media's War in the Persian Gulf: A Global Perspective*. Boulder, CO: Westview, 1992.

Ghareeb, Edmund. *Split Vision: The Portrayal of Arabs in the American Media*. Washington, D.C.: American-Arab Affairs Council, 1983.

Griswald, William J. *The Image of the Middle East in Secondary School Textbooks*. New York: Middle East Studies Association of North America, 1975.

Groot, Amy K. and Steven J. Rosen, eds. *The Campaign to Discredit Israel*. Washington, D.C.: American Israel Public Affairs Committee, 1983.

Haddad, Yvonne. "The Challenge of Muslim Minorityness: The American Experience." In *The Integration of Islam and Hinduism in Western Europe*. Ed. W. A. R. Shadid and P. S. van Koningsveld. Kampen: Kok Pharos, 1991.

Haddad, Yvonne Yazbeck and Adair T. Lummis. *Islamic Values in the United States: A Comparative Study*. New York: Oxford University Press, 1987.

Hagopian, E. and A. Paden, eds. *The Arab-Americans: Studies in Assimilation*. Wilmette, IL: Medina University Press International, 1969.

Hagopian, Elaine. "Minority Rights in a Nation State: The Nixon Administration's Campaign against Arab-Americans." *Journal of Palestine Studies* 5.1/2 (1975–76): 97–114.

Haney-López, Ian. *White by Law: The Legal Construction of Race*. New York: New York University Press, 1996.

Hathout, Maher. "Islamic Work in North America: Challenges and Opportunities." In Siddiqui.

Hitti, Philip Khuri. *The Syrians in America*. New York: George H. Doran Co., 1924.

Hoogland, Eric, ed. *Crossing the Waters: Arabic-Speaking Immigrants in the United States before 1940.* Washington, D.C.: Smithsonian Institution Press, 1987.

Hourani, Albert. *Western Attitudes Towards Islam.* Southampton: University of Southampton, 1974.

Hussaini, Hatem I. "The Impact of the Arab-Israeli Conflict on Arab Communities in the United States." In *Settler Regimes in Africa and the Arab World: The Illusion of Endurance.* Ed. Ibrahim Abu-Lughod and Baha Abu-Laban. Wilmette, IL: The Medina University Press International, 1974.

Jabara, Abdeen, "The FBI and the Civil Rights of Arab-Americans." *ADC Issues* no. 5 (n.d.): 1.

Jarrar, Samir Ahmad. "Images of the Arabs in United States Secondary School Textbooks." Diss., Florida State University, 1976.

Karim, Karim H. *Islamic Peril: Media and Global Violence.* Montreal: Black Rose Books, 2000.

Kettani, Muhammad Ali. *Muslim Minorities in the World Today.* London: Mansell, 1986.

Kiernan, V. G. *The Lords of Human Kind: European Attitudes to the Outside World in the Imperial Age.* London: Pelican, 1972.

Kramer, Martin. "Islam vs. Democracy." *Commentary* 95.1 (1993): 35–42.

Malek, Abbas. *Newsmedia and Foreign Relations: A Multi-faceted Perspective.* Norwood, NJ: Ablex Publishing, 1996.

Mawlana, Hamid, George Gerbner, and Herbert I Schiller, eds. *Triumph of the Image: The Media's War in the Persian Gulf–A Global Perspective.* Boulder, CO: Westview, 1992.

Mehdi, Mohammad T. *Of Lions Chained; An Arab Looks at America.* San Francisco: New World Press, 1962.

———. *Peace in Palestine.* New York: New World Press, 1976.

———. *Terrorism: Why America is the Target.* New York: New World Press, 1988.

Metcalf, Barbara D. "New Medinas: The Tablighi Jama'at in America and Europe." In *Making Muslim Space in North America and Europe.* Ed. Barbara Daly Metcalf. Berkeley: University of California Press, 1996.

Mokarzel, Salloum A. "Can We Retain our Heritage: A Call to Form a Federation of Syrian Societies." *Syrian World*, November 1928: 36–40.

Moore, Kathleen. *al-Mughtaribun: American Law and the Transformation of Muslim Life in the United States*. Albany: State University of New York Press, 1995.

Nadvi, Syed A. Hassan Ali. *Muslims in the West: The Message and Mission*. London: Islamic Foundation, 1983.

Neff, Alixa. *Becoming American: The Early Arab Immigrant Experience*. Carbondale: Southern Illinois University Press, 1985.

Orfalea, Gregory. "Sifting the Ashes: Arab-American Activism During the 1982 Invasion of Lebanon." *Arab Studies Quarterly* 11.2&3 (1989): 207–26.

Osman, Mohammad Fathi. "Towards a Vision and an Agenda for the Future of Muslim Ummah." In Siddiqui.

Palumbo, Michael. "Land Without a People" [online]. 1987. [cited 5/18/2003] *http://www.geocities.com/Capitolhill/Senate/7891Palumbo_chptr1.html*

Perry, Glenn. "Treatment of the Middle East in American High School Textbooks." *Journal of Palestine Studies* 4.3 (1975): 46–58.

Pipes, Daniel. "The Muslims are Coming! The Muslims are Coming!" *National Review*, November 19, 1990: 28–31.

Quraishi, M. Tareq. *Ismail al-Faruqi: An Enduring Legacy*. Plainfield, IN: The Muslim Student Association, 1987.

Qutb, Sayyid. *Milestones*. Indianapolis: American Trust, 1990.

Said, Edward. *Covering Islam: How the Media and the Experts Determine How We See the Rest of the World*. New York: Vantage Books, 1997.

Samhan, Helen Hatab. "Politics and Exclusion: The Arab American Experience." *Journal of Palestine Studies* 16.2 (1987): 11–28.

Sephardic Archives. *The Spirit of Aleppo: Syrian Jewish Immigrant Life in New York, 1890–1939*. Brooklyn, New York, 1986.

Shah, Mowahid. "The FBI and the Civil Rights of Arab-Americans." Washington, D.C.: ADC Research Institute, 1986.

Shaheen, Jack G. *Abscam: Arabiaphobia in America*. Washington, D.C.: American-Arab Anti-Discrimination Committee, 1980.

——. *Arab and Muslim Stereotyping in American Popular Culture*. Washington, D.C.: Center for Muslim Christian Understanding, 1997.

——. *Reel Bad Arabs: How Hollywood Vilifies a People*. New York: Olive Branch Press, 2001.

——. *The TV Arab*. Bowling Green: The Popular Press, 1984.

Siddiqui, Muhammad Ahmadullah, ed. *Islam: A Contemporary Perspective*. Chicago: NAAMPS, 1994.

Simon, Reeva S. *The Middle East in Crime Fiction: Mysteries, Spy Novels, and Thrillers from 1916 to the 1980s*. New York: Lilian Barber Press, 1989.

Steet, Linda. *Veils and Daggers: A Century of National Geographic's Representation of the Arab World*. Philadelphia: Temple University, 2000.

Suleiman, Michael. "Early Arab-Americans: The Search for Identity." In Hoogland.

Terry, Janice J. *Mistaken Identity: Arab Stereotypes in Popular Writing*. Washington, D.C.: American-Arab Affairs Council, 1985.

Tolan, John V. *Saracens: Islam in the Medieval European Imagination*. New York: Columbia University Press, 2002.

U.S. Department of State. "Muslim Life in America" [online]. Washington, D.C.: Office of International Information Programs, U.S. Department of State, 2003. [cited 5/15/2003] Available at *http://usinfo.state.gov/products/pubs/muslimlife*.

Vaux, Kenneth I. *Ethics and the Gulf War: Religion, Rhetoric, and Righteousness*. Boulder, CO: Westview, 1992.

Young, Robert. *White Mythologies: Writing History and the West*. London: Routledge, 1990.

Zenner, Walter B. "The Syrian Jews of Brooklyn." In *A Community of Many Worlds: Arab Americans in New York City*. Ed. Kathleen Benson and Philip M. Kayal. Syracuse: Syracuse University Press, 2002.

Previous Charles Edmondson Historical Lecturers

*Paul K. Conkin, University of Wisconsin, 1977–1978: "American Christianity in Crisis: Religious Rationalism and Darwinism."

*Walter LaFeber, Cornell University, 1979–1980: "The Third Cold War: Kissinger Years and Carter Years."

*Martin E. Marty, University of Chicago, 1980–1981: "Religious Crises in Modern America: Modernism and Fundamentalism."

**William H. McNeill, University of Chicago, 1981–1982: "The Great Frontier: Freedom and Hierarchy in Modern Times."

Robert L. Heilbroner, The New School for Social Research, 1982–1983: "Capitalism in Transition: The Twentieth Century."

C. Vann Woodward, Yale University, emeritus, 1983–1984: "Continuing Themes in Southern History: *The Strange Career of Jim Crow*, 1954–1984; and *The Burden of Southern History*, 1952–1984"

*William E. Leuchtenburg, University of North Carolina, Chapel Hill, 1984–1985: "The 1984 Presidential Election in Historical Perspective: From Civil War to the New Deal; From Franklin Roosevelt to Ronald Reagan."

Peter Gay, Yale University, 1985–1986: "Aggression: Toward a Theory of Aggression," and "Humor: Aggression at Work."

*Gordon S. Wood, Brown University, 1986–1987: The Making of the Constitution."

Gerder Lerner, University of Wisconsin, Madison, 1987–1988: "Sex and Class: A Revisionist Perspective."

*Robert Darnton, Princeton University, 1988–1989: "The French Revolution at Street Level" and "From Enlightenment to Revolution."

*Stephen B. Oates, University of Massachusetts, 1989–1990: "Biography: The Heart of History" and "How the Trumpet Came to Sound: The Process and Perils of Writing a Biography of Martin Luther King, Jr."

*Dan T. Carter, Emory University 1990–1991: "George Wallace, Richard Nixon, and the Transformation of American Politics."

*Geoffrey A. Hosking, University of London, 1991–1992: "Empire and Nation in Russian History."

*Nell Irvin Painter, Princeton University, 1992–1993: "Soul Murder and Slavery."

*Philip D. Curtin, Johns Hopkins University, 1993–1994: "Why People Move: Migration in African History."

*Franklin W. Knight, Johns Hopkins University, 1994–1995: "Race, Class, and Ethnicity in Latin American and the Caribbean."

*Jonathan D. Spence, Yale University, 1995–1996: "The Taiping Vision of a Christian China, 1836–1864."

*David N. Cannadine, Columbia University, 1996–1997: "Britain in Decline?"

*Alan Brinkley, Columbia University, 1997–1998: "Culture and Politics in the Great Depression."

Leon F. Litwack, University of California, Berkeley, 1998–1999: "Wade in the Water: African Americans and Race Relations."

*Geoffrey Parker, Ohio State University, 1999–2000: "The World is Not Enough: The Imperial Vision of Philip II of Spain."

Linda Kerber, University of Iowa, 2000–2001: "Gender and Inequality."

*Yvonne Haddad, Georgetown University, 2001–2002: "Not Quite Americans? The Shaping of Arab and Muslim Identity in the United States."

Gary B. Nash, University of California, Los Angeles, 2002–2003: "Imagining Life in the Americas."

*David J. Weber, Southern Methodist University, 2003–2004: "Spanish Bourbons and Wild Indians."

*Printed copies are available from Baylor University Press
**Printed copies are available from Princeton University Press